# HOW TO HUMAN

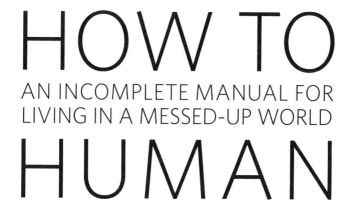

# HOW TO

## AN INCOMPLETE MANUAL FOR
## LIVING IN A MESSED-UP WORLD

# HUMAN

**ALICE CONNOR**

Fortress Press

Minneapolis

To all the humans in the world who need a manual:
this may or may not be it.

make some coffee
wash the dishes from the night before
don't get overwhelmed by the
vastness of the world as you
try to find your place in it
—"Daily Activities," Suze Shore


The greats weren't great because
at first they could paint;
The greats were great because
they painted a lot.
—"Ten Thousand Hours,"
Macklemore and Ryan Lewis

# TABLE OF CONTENTS

Introduction: Try It, You'll Like It . . . . . . . . . . . . . . . . . . . . . . .xi

1. Take People Seriously . . . . . . . . . . . . . . . . . . . . . . . . . . . . 3

2. Do Shit on Purpose . . . . . . . . . . . . . . . . . . . . . . . . . . . . . 17

3. Sucking at Something Is the First Step to Being
   Sorta Good at Something . . . . . . . . . . . . . . . . . . . . . . . . 31

4. Take Off the Costume . . . . . . . . . . . . . . . . . . . . . . . . . . . 45

5. If It's Not Okay, It's Not the End . . . . . . . . . . . . . . . . . . . . 57

6. It's Okay to Feel Your Feelings . . . . . . . . . . . . . . . . . . . . . 69

7. Say the Thing . . . . . . . . . . . . . . . . . . . . . . . . . . . . . . . . 83

8. Ask for What You Need . . . . . . . . . . . . . . . . . . . . . . . . . . 95

9. You're Involved, Not in Control . . . . . . . . . . . . . . . . . . . 109

10. If We Eat Together, We Will Not Betray
    One Another . . . . . . . . . . . . . . . . . . . . . . . . . . . . . . . . 121

11. Consider the Lilies, Dammit . . . . . . . . . . . . . . . . . . . . . . 133

12. Ambiguity Is Neither Good nor Bad . . . . . . . . . . . . . . . 145

13. Everything's Awkward. Lean into It . . . . . . . . . . . . . . . . 157

Conclusion: So What?. . . . . . . . . . . . . . . . . . . . . . . . . . . . . . . 169

Thank Yous . . . . . . . . . . . . . . . . . . . . . . . . . . . . . . . . . . . . . . . . 175

Appendix: Further Proof . . . . . . . . . . . . . . . . . . . . . . . . . . . . 177

Notes . . . . . . . . . . . . . . . . . . . . . . . . . . . . . . . . . . . . . . . . . . . . . . 183

# INTRODUCTION: TRY IT, YOU'LL LIKE IT

> People don't really want to
> be cured. What they want
> is relief; a cure is painful.
> —Anthony de Mello, *Awareness*

Listen, my parents are amazing cooks. My dad wooed my mom back in the day by making her authentic French food and my mom has spent months perfecting handmade puff pastry and delicious, moist layer cakes. Eating at their house is a joy. Mostly. When my brother and I were kids, our parents tried to get us to eat all kinds of things—"I'm not a short-order cook," they'd say, "This is what we're eating." Whenever they cooked something new, they'd say, "Try it, you'll like it." Sometimes they'd say it in a sing-song voice, as though that would make the lima beans or enchiladas or scallops more enticing. I'd spend an hour at the table staring at that one lonely scallop or forkful of limas I had to eat before being excused, watching it turn unappetizingly cold. I didn't want to try something new: it was disgusting and frightening.

My little child brain tested out all sorts of hypotheses at that dinner table. I thought, "If I sit here long enough, they'll let me leave the table without eating it," and, "If I eat it really fast and try not to let it touch my tongue, it'll taste better." Nope and nope. I thought, "I've never had this before, so it must be gross." That one doesn't even hold up logically. Most of the things I tried, I did indeed like—collard greens, sushi, Javanese pork— and so forgot about the fear. Scallops even, I discovered as an adult, are mind-meltingly delicious when fresh and seared in butter and salt and pepper.

"Try it, you'll like it" is another way of saying that life is really a series of experiments. First, observe things. When I sit in the tub, the water level rises. When someone asks if I need help, I immediately say no even if I need it. Second, ask a question. Why does the water level rise? Why do I reject help? Third, form a hypothesis. Matter added to liquid displaces an equal volume of liquid. If I accept help, it makes me look weak. Fourth, experiment. Add different items to water and measure the water displaced. Spend a day saying yes to everyone who offers help and notice weakness levels. And fifth, reflect on what you've learned. I was right about the matter displacing water and wrong about looking weak. Observe, question, hypothesize, act, reflect.

The more we practice this kind of experimentation, the more we learn. Do a thing, reflect on how well it went and what you learned, then go out and do it again, this time with more wisdom behind it. Action, reflection, action. Our actions are more compassionate and fruitful when we pay attention to them. But we can't spend our entire lives just thinking about things; we've got to walk the path back and forth between action and reflection. Just try it, my parents' voices say, you'll like it. Looking at your life as an experiment rather than as written in stone is so freeing because it means there is always possibility.

Experimentation is not about having the right answer but about having options. It's about seeing the mess of the world and trying various things to do something about it. And it can be fun. Experiments are the adult version of playing, where anything is possible and you're practicing things that will be helpful later. There's no right answer to being human, the title of this book notwithstanding. This book is about spiritual experimentation and, in particular, about my laboratory: the Edge House campus ministry at the University of Cincinnati.

When I started at the Edge House, we had a lovely, rambling house, a truly terrible website, and no students. I was restarting a community that had petered out, and the house had been empty for two years: all the possibilities were before us. Ten years later, the house is even more lovely, the website is much better, and, depending on how you count, we have six hundred students. We grow vegetables and make bread and pour really great coffee and give it all away. We swear and play nerdy board games. I go into the offices of people I've never met just to say, "Hello, I'm here if you need me. What's up in your life?" We have regular dinners, group conversations, and worship centered around honest, difficult questions to help us be better humans.

My students and I put wheels on a red couch (cleverly called "the Red Couch") and set it up on campus every few weeks like a mini living room with a rug, a side chair, and a floor lamp that doesn't plug into anything. The A-frame chalkboard we take with us has various pithy and sweary invitations to talk on it. We value curiosity and vulnerability over and against defensiveness and rigidity. We are unabashedly universalist and value doubt and atheism as much as strong belief, so we interact with the campus with no agenda other than relationship. We don't try to convert or judge people, no matter where they are on a spectrum of belief, so the conversations are usually quite jovial. We're not perfect, so obviously, we fail a lot.

We talk with the people who come by the Red Couch about Saturday morning cartoons and deciding what to do with the rest of their lives. We talk about how to be good romantic or sexual partners and about how messy and difficult the Bible is. We talk about how to live a life of kindness in a world that tells us kindness is stupid. We talk to students and staff, conservatives and liberals, white people and people of color, straight people, gay people, trans people, rich people, poor people, all the people. And every conversation makes us more compassionate to the next person.

When we're out on the Red Couch, people want to air their grievances, but just as often, they want to give voice to their pain. Once, a student approached to talk about why we had the F-bomb on the chalkboard since we're Christians. "Why would you advertise that? You're leading people astray." We good-naturedly argued for a bit about whether it was okay to swear, and I eventually asked him about his schoolwork and how he was doing. We talked for much longer about his tendency to procrastinate and his uncertainty about his career. Instead of seeing each other as adversaries, we were able to talk together about our pain—his about not having the tenacity to do what needed to be done, mine about fear of failure. It's hard to have these conversations and be vulnerable with people we love, much less strangers (or, perhaps for you, it's the other way around), but trying it out leads to more possibilities than hiding and assuming.

    Being a human is hard, and it's because we are all wounded. When we were children and we first learned that the world didn't love us unconditionally, it hurt. And it kept hurting. Whether it was something obvious like abuse or abandonment or something smaller with a slow buildup, we tried to protect ourselves from the pain. We wrapped ourselves in layers of protection, like a cartoon hospital patient covered with so much surgical gauze they can't move, only we've done it to our emotions, to our spirit. We don't want other people to see this festering wound we carry around inside us or, God forbid, touch it. What would they say? They'd run away, probably. Or, worse, they'd try to fix it. I know it hurts, but I'd rather wallow in the pain I know than reach for the recovery that might hurt more. We've wrapped ourselves in so many layers of protection, much of the time we don't even know what that wound is to begin with; we've hidden it from our own selves.

And yet we can still feel it: something is deeply wrong. We can see with our own two eyes the world is messed up—though some trustworthy people say it's a little less so now than it has been. How do we respond to the suffering of people harassed and killed by police? What do we make of leaders, whether we chose them or not, who lie on the daily to deflect blame? What should we do when our brother or child or aunt lashes out? The institutions we love are dying, darkness hems us in, and we're all afraid of each other for any number of reasons.

This is essentially the point of the book: the world is a mess right now, and the only way to make it better is to listen to and be painfully honest with each other, especially with people we find repugnant. It's just that simple. If we can find the gumption to take someone seriously who represents everything we can't understand and can't abide, suddenly they're human, suddenly we're human. Embrace doubt, failure, ambiguity, and vulnerability, because in doing so, everything changes. Seriously. What seemed impossible is now accessible. What seemed permanent is now transient. This is not naïve, no matter how many centuries we've made a hobby of hurting each other. It's not some bullshit PC thing; political correctness is only a regimented version of empathy, kindness through language, a concept misunderstood

by both the left and the right. And it's not a reprimand or sham-
ing either. It's an invitation to trying something new.

To get at all this wisdom, each chapter focuses on a concept
we practice at the Edge House and includes a kind of spiritual
experiment you could try. Most of the time, these are things we
literally say out loud to each other, other times, they're descrip-
tive of behavior. You'll notice that the chapters overlap a bit in
how I talk about their subjects because our brains and souls
aren't so easily described. It's kind of like a big, thirteen-part
Venn diagram with sections of each chapter overlapping sections of others. And as you read the stories in each chapter,
know that I changed many people's names to allow for their
privacy.

You might feel uncomfortable reading this book. Trying
new things and breaking out of the bandages we have wrapped
around ourselves is frightening. Recovery looks threatening
because it's not what we're used to, and there's a certain comfort in the pain we know. Yet, intentionally stepping over the
barriers we've set up is empowering and liberating. The proverb writers warn us about the grass on the other side of the
fence, but sometimes it really is greener over there. The Twitter
user known as Garbage Oprah writes, "Sure sex is great, but
have you ever started tending to your childhood wound as an
empathic and competent adult?"[1]

I recently learned about this thing that happens to astronauts when they get to space called the overview effect. Apparently, all of them feel this to some extent or another. When they

get into space, when they finally get outside the pull of gravity and take a moment to turn around, everything changes. They see firsthand the little ball of Earth hanging in space and understand immediately, in their guts, its fragility and the tenuousness of the thin envelope of atmosphere surrounding it. The Wikipedia article says, "From space, national boundaries vanish, the conflicts that divide people become less important, and the need to create a planetary society with the united will to protect this 'pale blue dot' becomes both obvious and imperative."

One article I read says that in looking back at the Earth, astronauts can attain a similar spiritual experience to meditating Buddhist monks. These astronauts—scientists and soldiers—have a transcendent spiritual experience recognizing that we are all part of this one, delicately balanced whole. They can't look at human life or politics or any of the -isms we've made up the same way again. I will never go to space and have this experience, partly because I get violently ill on airplanes, but I've had similar experiences at other points in my life—at the tops of mountains, at the births of my children. Perhaps you have, too.

Being a better human means practicing kindness, honesty, and awareness. You might like it. It's okay to be afraid; it will only change your life.

# 1

# Take People Seriously

> I think if we could see each other as
> God sees us, the beauty would be
> too much. To see the dignity and the
> value and the beauty of every single
> person? Could we bear to look?
> —The Reverend Heidi Johns, my boss

I met Jesus in a gas-station parking lot. Bought him a cup of coffee.

I'd popped down the street from the Edge House to our local minimart to pick up a couple gallons of whole milk for lattes. I was grabbing the door handle to go in when I heard shoes scraping the pavement and turned to look. He was a very put-together middle-aged man, dressed in a suit and tie with a trench coat over his arm, his skin dark and smooth, pulling a wheeled suitcase with a broken handle. He was muttering angrily about schedules and timing. He looked like he was about to cry. I asked if he was okay. He looked at me, and his face opened up like a gift. He said, "I'm Jesus Christ and my father's abandoned me and I don't know why."

He went on, always on the verge of sobbing, about how he came down off the cross and someone else died there in his place and Peter and John and all wouldn't talk to him. He talked about how his father, God, was cruel to him and also how much he loved his father. I noticed that he wasn't as put together as I'd thought. His suit was badly frayed at the cuffs and around the collar, his white shirt unevenly ivory from wear, and also, he was obviously not Jesus of Nazareth.

But at my previous church, we referred to folks who came to the door asking for help with rent or gas or food as Jesus. "Where's Father Jim?" "He's talking to Jesus." It wasn't snide or mocking but a reminder that Jesus told us over and over that he's with these folks, that he *is* these folks. As sad and predictable as their stories can be, as frustrating as the system whose cracks they've fallen through is, they're still people. They need help, these people we would just as soon pass by and continue on our merry way. They bear the face of God in a mystical way, and sometimes we're paying attention and see it.

So, I bought my new friend Jesus Christ a cup of gas-station coffee, listened to his story, and he walked away. He didn't once ask for anything, just wanted to talk about his pain. I felt off-balance. I hadn't been expecting to meet Jesus. I hadn't been expecting to give some of my time to this suffering man on the way to pick up milk. I hadn't been expecting to feel lighter and more connected because of it, especially since I couldn't solve his problem. But I did. He didn't dismiss me because I'm a lady priest with tattoos, and I didn't dismiss him because he looked a little shabby and saw things I didn't. He was beautiful in the midst of his melancholy delusion, and I was surprised and surprisingly serene because of it.

When I visit local churches to talk about college ministry, the primary question I get is, "What do the young people want these days?" What they usually mean is one of two things: "How can we get more young people in our doors and giving us money without changing anything?" or, "I love this community and tradition, and I'm really worried that what I love will disintegrate." I hear similar things at political party meetings, school boards, hell, I bet the Kiwanis Club, too. I'm here to tell you, they're not going to participate without changing things, and everything we adults love will disintegrate eventually. That is the way of things. But I'm also here to tell you, the kids are alright. And they're damn perceptive. They can tell we don't take them seriously.

Our culture disdains millennials and Gen Z because of their age. It's ridiculous, the number of articles about how millennials are killing the paper-napkin industry or the fabric-softener industry, and how, egad, they're waiting longer to get married so they can get to know each other better and that's why Toys R Us closed. I hear older adults talk about how lazy these young people are, how absurd their obsessions with the Snapchats and the avocado toasts. Young people struggle to pay for college and to find jobs that pay a decent wage. My students talk about what they're passionate about—permaculture, neuroscience, social justice, universal education—only to receive a figurative pat on the head or a horrified "But . . . but that's socialism" from people older than they are. They even have a term for their necessary part-time jobs: side-hustle. They are hustling like their lives depend on it, because they do. Their multiple side-hustles put together might make a full-time job, or they might not.

It's not just a millennial or Gen Z thing—every older generation has treated the younger folks with, at best, condescension. I'm firmly Gen X and grew up being told "you are the future!" and having adults heap praise on me. But when I spoke up for justice and the environment, I was shut down because I was too young to know what I was talking about. After the Marjory Stoneman Douglas High School mass shooting in 2018, so many commentators said the survivors were too young to have an opinion about gun control, even as they're plenty old enough to vote and work and join the military. And apparently they're old enough to be shot. We spend our children's entire lives preparing them to be independent, giving them novels to read and movies to watch where the scrappy, young protagonists fight violent, overbearing authorities, and we don't recognize that we are that authority they're declaring their independence from.

Because we don't look at them as full people, we don't take them seriously.

This is the origin of Black Lives Matter and related movements: they're not saying, "Only black lives matter," they're saying, "Black lives matter, *too.*" They're saying it because their experience is that their lives haven't mattered. At all. Whether it's because of 246 years of the American slave trade, 89 years of segregation and Jim Crow, or 50 years of working for civil rights when they still fear for their lives at traffic stops or in their own damn backyards talking on a cell phone, we as a culture are not taking them seriously. Their pain is real. Their pain is difficult to see when we haven't experienced it. Their pain is inconvenient. If white folks like me choose to really see it, we have to stop, like the good Samaritan on the road to Jericho, and do what we can to heal the wounded. It means we have to listen when they tell us their stories, not just cover our discomfort with platitudes or justifications.

When it comes to politics and religion, no one takes each other seriously. Whatever group we belong to is the right one, the righteous one, and anyone else is at least deluded if not outright evil. It's because our brains are still wired for fight or flight, even though there's no saber-toothed tiger in front of us to fight or flee. The tiger we have to confront is our own self-interest. We don't stop to consider that other people's experiences are just as legitimate as our own. Why would we? We're right. It feeds on itself, this unwillingness to allow for even the possibility of understanding.

Women's experiences are dismissed, especially in health settings. My own beloved grandmother, an emergency-room nurse, used to tell me my motion sickness was all in my head. I'd say to myself, "Maybe, but it's also about to be all over your shoes." So many women have stories about asking their doctor what a symptom means and being condescended to or disbelieved that a lot of us stopped speaking up.

Transgender folks are constantly misgendered and assaulted because of their identities. A scientific study just came out saying trans folks are happier and more productive when the people around them accept their trans identity. No shit. They've been saying it for years. Immigrants are separated from their children and told they're nothing, that they're animals. People with mental illness are afraid to ask for help because our culture says it's all weakness or criminal or not even real at all.

Taking each other seriously doesn't mean agreeing with each other on every point. We are not homogenized people, like milk. We're more like pineapple-orange juice with added vitamin D and lots of pulp, maybe a few seeds for good measure. Of course we have different opinions on what makes a good movie and what constitutes a just war or a stable family. Disagreeing doesn't require that one of us is wrong or less than. Taking each other seriously does mean choosing to see each other's pain and experiences as real. It means choosing to be compassionate, especially when people are mystifying and inconvenient. It means recognizing the dignity of every human being, simply because they are human beings.

Do you remember Eeyore in *Winnie-the-Pooh*? He's the stuffed donkey who's always grumpy and depressed. You might think he'd be a huge downer to his friends—and maybe he is, we don't know their thoughts—but they're still friends with him. He's a beloved member of their little community, and they go out of their way to include him, rescue him, care for him. His depression isn't a barrier to relationship. His friends take him seriously; they love him for everything about him.

This is really difficult. This chapter is kind of a first among equals: you can step into the stream of becoming a better human at any point along its course, and one of the primary requirements to do so is to regard the people around you as actually people. Call this your swim fins for the shallow end of the river. For people to be actually people—not a caricature or an assumption based on social media or your dad's pontificating—for people to be actually people, we have to choose to see them as they are, not as we think they ought to be.

When I started the Edge House, a couple of the first people in the community were two law students, self-described conservatives, who were articulate, thoughtful, and compassionate. Their presence with us, their willingness to challenge the predominant, self-satisfied liberal campus perspective in reasoned ways, shaped our community for good. One of our core values continues to be an openness to all perspectives, a willingness to listen for the soul of the person, not just for the argument to be had. I could have tried to convince them to be good liberals like me. I could have scoffed at their values or mocked them, as is apparently now the standard of discourse. But instead, we welcomed them to our table, embraced them as siblings and comrades, asked them questions, and tried to understand.

We even learned to see where we agreed on some things, shocking as that may seem. One of those students and I have argued, in a loving and respectful way, about small government versus big government for years now. We've also argued about the origins and purpose of feminism, really since the day we met. Just the other day, I realized how close our perspectives were and immediately messaged him. What if his desire for small government and my commitment to feminism arise from the same good place: letting people choose how they want to exist in the world rather than being told what they have to do. I call this *let me do my thing*. Let me be a woman the way I want to be, and you be a man the way you want to be, without any expectation of roles. Let us all make financial and vocational decisions without so much babysitting. This moment of deeper understanding between us wouldn't have happened if we hadn't taken each other so seriously, and if we hadn't chosen to look at each other with love.

Here's another story: in 1993 in Minneapolis, a teenager named Oshea Israel murdered Mary Johnson's son Laramiun Byrd. Near the end of Oshea's sixteen-year sentence, Mrs. Johnson went to visit him. She wanted to look him in the eye, see if he'd changed at all. He had, and when you hear her tell her story, it's obvious that she changed as well. After they'd talked about her son for a while, she stood up and hugged Oshea, the man who'd murdered her son. She realized she'd forgiven him. Now, even curiouser, they live next door to each other. He takes out her trash. She cooks dinner for him. And she takes as much pride in his college graduation as she would have for her own son's, the son he murdered. It's an unlikely relationship. Most of us take pleasure in the suffering of our enemies, which is in turn another form of violence. Oshea and Mary resist the culture's expectation; they live lives of dignity and curious respect. They chose to see each other differently.

As I said, taking each other seriously doesn't mean agreeing all the time. My father and I used to argue a lot, and I'd say, "You don't understand, let me try again," and he'd say, "No, I understand just fine. I don't agree." Listening to a freshman who's just discovered the men's rights movement bloviate about legalizing rape doesn't mean I affirm what he's saying; it means I recognize his innate humanity and wonder where his pain comes from. Listening to a trans-excluding radical feminist talk about the immutability of biological sex doesn't mean I agree with what she's saying; it means I choose to look at her with compassion as I hope she would at me, and wonder how this opinion serves her or her relationships.

There is possibility here, there is open space we can walk into together and really see each other and be seen. There is freedom in admitting that we don't know everything and that other people have something to teach us. Curiosity—as opposed to judgment or defensiveness—is the doorway we walk through to possibility and freedom. In embracing all of these things, we begin to find the parts of ourselves we've misplaced; we become more complete humans.

On campus, one of the largest problems we have is how to hear people's stories when we disagree with them. Whether it's street preachers or arguments about how sexual assault should be handled, we need a way to move through the problem instead of dancing around it or throwing words like rotten fruit at each other. The university is meant to be both a place of experimentation and challenge as well as a safe space from slurs and gender- or race-based violence. It's meant to welcome the whole person. The problem is we've begun to conflate *safe* with *comfortable*. As conflict arises, we get more extreme in our thinking: people who need these safe spaces begin to believe that they deserve to be safe from being offended as well as physically safe, and people who think safe spaces are ridiculous mock the people who need them.

There's a huge difference between being uncomfortable and being unsafe. Caring for each other is not about hiding from things we dislike, it's about being safe enough to hear another person and to experiment with listening and choosing. Safety is strangely the primary need for risk-taking. We need to feel safe in one part of our lives so that we can take a risk somewhere else. Parenting is about setting boundaries like good bedtimes and limited screen-time—not to control or manipulate our children, but because good boundaries instill in them a strong sense of safety. The safer they feel, the more likely they'll make friends on the playground and risk following their dreams to become a zoologist or acrobat or civil servant.

The best of all possible worlds is that we get excited to learn more about our neighbors. I've got a recent graduate, Nathan, whose spiritual gift is being thrilled for other people. Someone comes into the Edge House with good news, and he jumps up to do a happy dance with them. When one of our students got a job she'd been hoping for, he walked down to the bakery and bought her a cake. He doesn't want to do the job she got, and he doesn't necessarily understand all the nuance of what someone else's good news is, but he's excited for them nonetheless.

I heard a story about a guy a while back who was a huge hit at parties. He was the most in-demand party guest. People loved him. What made him so interesting was this: he asked people what they did for a living, and when they told him, he said, "Wow. That sounds hard." They'd open right up. "Oh my gosh, it is! Thank you for noticing!" and they'd be off to the races.[2] Really, we only want to be heard.

So, let's try an experiment. Start small. Choose someone you know you'll interact with today or, if you prefer, let this interaction arise organically. When you run into them, look them in the eye. If it's appropriate, shake hands or hug or put your hand on their shoulder. Ask them how they are. Then, and this is key, really listen to what they say. Don't assume, don't just wait to say your thing, don't pretend. Ask them clarifying questions. You can say things like, "What does that mean?" or

"Interesting. Tell me more." This is what we in the business call *small talk*, but it's different; it's small talk with a purpose. The purpose is to see the other person's value as they are. The purpose is to see what happens if you really listen, in the conversation and inside you.

You can take this a step further and ask yourself questions about things you see in the news or on social media. Who wrote the story you're seeing? Who benefits from that particular story? Who or what is missing from it? Ask these questions from a place of curiosity, not cynicism; from wonder, not judgment.

What's funny about this experiment is it works to shut down misogynists and racists as well. If you're really paying attention to them, taking seriously what they say and asking where it comes from, it makes them think, it makes them stumble. You could get all schadenfreude about it, but when we stumble, when our assumptions fail us, that's when we change. When someone's worldview fails them, we can be there to catch them, to offer safety and love.

If we come at our conversations from a place of loving curiosity, they start to look different, and we start to look different. The beauty of asking about someone else's story is that it changes us as well—it makes us more complete.

# 2

# Do Shit on Purpose

One step, one punch,
one round at a time.
—Rocky Balboa, *Creed* (2015)

Our first apartment as a newly married couple in Columbus was terrible. It had a lovely view of the gas station and the back parking lot of the Chinese sports bar across the street. When the neighbors' bathroom sprung a leak that ended up in our kitchen, the handyman grudgingly replaced all the cabinets but just painted over the black mold on the wall behind them. He fixed a long crack in a window with clear caulk. It was shit, but it was ours.

I got permission from the landlady to plant a garden along two sides of the apartment. I put in tomatoes, sweet william,

Siberian iris, cleome, and a truly unfortunate amount of purple basil. It was everywhere. There was a little stone path to get across it onto the lawn and a smiling stone face peeking out from behind a boxwood. It was not the kind of garden that would grace the cover of *Fancy Homes* or anything, but I made it and I loved it. I would work out there for hours, weeding mostly and getting sweaty and itchy, sometimes just staring at it for minutes on end, eyes unfocused, cup of tea growing cold in my hands, imagining what else I'd do. It's a look gardeners get sometimes.

After a few hours out there and covered in dirt, I'd pop inside and ask my husband, Leighton, to come see what I'd wrought. He'd come out and say, "Wow, it's amazing! It looks so intentional." I know, no one else talks like that in real life, and it sounds sarcastic, especially if you could hear his voice, Mr. No-One-Can-Tell-When-I'm-Being-Sincere. But it's what he said, and it was entirely complimentary. You could tell I'd been there, because things looked different. For something to look intentional rather than accidental was brilliant. It didn't have to look *good*, just intended.

At our second house, the pattern continued. We bought this lovely little bungalow on a lovely street from a lovely lady, and I immediately started digging. Raspberries and tansy and red-hot pokers in the front, hostas and azaleas in the back. It was glorious. There were lots of moments of calling the sarcastic husband outside to admire what I'd done to the yard on purpose.

At this house, there was a narrow strip of land between our property and the neighbors' behind us that I think technically belonged to them but was entirely blocked from their view by a fence and their garage. It was separated from us by a rusty chain-link fence. This forlorn patch of ground, maybe three feet deep by twenty feet wide, just sat there, chock-full of weeds, for years. I could see it but couldn't get to it. One summer, I finally clambered over the fence to start weeding.

Turns out, previous owners on both sides of the fence had used it as a dumping ground for construction materials. There was a huge lump of dried concrete, heavy as hell, and a deeply buried pile of broken glass windowpanes—found those with my fingertips. Bits of metal and long pieces of wire, plastic bags, rotting boards, not to mention the small weeds that had turned into trees over the years and grown through the fence. People long before me just knocked the tops off the stupid pokeweed that kept coming up. Those things get enormous, and they're hard to get rid of once they drop their seeds. I finally got out a trowel to pull it up by the roots. The trowel was not enough. The shovel was barely enough. The root, when I finally, triumphantly dug it up, was the size of a mole. I'm not even kidding.

The rest of the yard was shaping up nicely, with a low retaining wall and curved beds with shade-loving plants—it was my pride and joy, a haven in a difficult world. But that no-man's-land—no one thought about it, it just happened.

Most of us go through our lives this same way, asleep, things just happening to us. We're alive, we're physically present, but we are unconscious and dreaming of other things. We don't see our patterns of behavior, we don't notice how our physical sensations signify something beyond pain and pleasure. The prefrontal cortex in our brain tricks us into thinking that we're in charge and choosing things rationally, but that's mostly a lie. Sometimes our dreams are so real, so vivid, we don't know they're not until we wake up. So it is when we're physically awake: everything seems so real, and we don't see that we're still spiritually asleep.

There's a reason some people of color use the word *woke* to describe awareness of institutionalized racism and unconscious bias—those things are symptoms of sleepwalking through life. They happen without our meaning them to, and we get defensive when they're brought up. "I didn't make them happen; I'm not actively oppressing anyone!" But we're also not actively trying to stop them either. A lot of the time, we don't even notice the systems around us that hurt people, because we aren't the ones being hurt by them. We're asleep. Waking up to what's happening around us is a difficult, painful process. I don't want to see my complicity in America's race or class or gender problems or my own violent responses to everyday frustrations. I resist waking up—my spiritual bed is so cozy, and it's such hard work to do shit intentionally.

It's not just massive institutional or political scenarios we're snoozing through. Staying asleep shows up in small things as well. When I ask my nine-year-old what she did in school and she says, "I don't know," it's because she's asleep to her day, her attention is elsewhere. She may or may not have been paying a lot of attention in class, but in the moment I ask her, she's thinking about something else: a snack, who to play with, something exciting coming up the next day. At the Edge House, when there's milk residue on the steam wand of our fancy espresso machine, it's because one of our trained baristas, who definitely knows better, wasn't paying attention. In our relationships and professional lives, when things go wrong, we say, "I couldn't help it," or "It just happened," or "Mistakes were made." No shit, Sherlock—by whom? What looks like conscious self-protection is often another form of being asleep—I don't really know how and why this thing happened. I wasn't paying attention.

We don't know it at the time, but we all grow up with a script that defines how we live our lives. Every family has one. It tells you what a clean house looks like and whether you write thank-you notes. Your script tells you how to interact with people. Your script tells you what holiday celebrations are supposed to look like. Your script tells you whether to stand up for yourself in an argument or whether to hide because you're in danger. It might be a loving, encouraging script or a lonely, fearful one. The script that we learn to enact in our families isn't necessarily morally good or bad, it just describes for us how to be a person. It tells us where our attention is supposed to be. Those of us with kids worry about whether they'll listen to us and the hopes we have for them. They are absolutely listening to us, but what they take from what they hear may not be what we intend. Even when the script is abusive, we learn how to respond to it—to acquiesce to power or to fight against it, and what happens when we do. We don't realize we have these scripts until we bump up against other people's. It slowly dawns on us that other people do things differently. Your family does *what* at Christmas? Why are you so upset about how I wash dishes? Why do you flinch when I get angry?

College-age folks are feverishly revising their scripts, whether they're aware of it or not. They've come from a particular way of doing things and have already begun questioning it (this is what all the drama is about in high school—it's not flippant self-interest, it's exploration). They might throw out the entire script and write a new one. They might heavily edit it or do little experiments here and there. Trans students might express more of the gender they feel. Tough guys might drink more or ignore their better instincts when a girl is wasted at a party. Or they might discover a deep well of emotion and experiment with being vulnerable with other men. Another student might be honest with herself about what she really wants to do with her life and change majors two years in. These young adults might experience something beautiful or traumatic that changes their whole perspective on the script they grew up with.

When we move out or go to college, it's a huge breakup with childhood, and there's usually a moment when we suddenly realize we're adults—bought our very own nail-clipper or talked to the financial-aid folks by ourselves. With this realization comes the first iteration of the question every one of us asks over and over: who will I be? This right here, this question, is the beginning of waking up. What kind of person will I be? How do I do that? What choices do I need to make? What mistakes will I make? It's entirely possible to change things, to revise our scripts, to become freer. To do that requires intention.

When one of our students, Dessa, told me she was struggling with narcotics addiction, I was surprised, but I was so proud of her for seeing what was happening in her brain and body and for getting the help she needed. She was so distraught—worried I'd judge her, worried about her classes, worried about how she was going to get out of the hole she'd dug. She asked me not to share the specifics with the Edge House community but said I could tell them she was sick. She went home for rehab and counseling—working the twelve steps helped her see the spiritual pain she'd been trying to numb. Over the year she was gone, we talked here and there. She returned to Cincinnati a new woman, with a new vocabulary and a new vitality, if not the perfect grasp of intentionality we hoped for.

And then she relapsed. It happens, more often than you'd think. Often enough that one of the slogans in some twelve-step groups is "relapse is a part of recovery." Obviously, you don't want to relapse, but you shouldn't let it stop your recovery. It's part of the process. Why do we fall? So we can learn to pick ourselves up. Dessa could have given up, said, "The hell with it. I've already messed this up, why not just give in?" She could have disappeared from our community or from her family. She didn't; she went back to the group and to rehab. And this time, when she returned, it was with a different kind of newness—a newness colored with humility and intentionality. She knew she couldn't do it on her own; she knew she had to prioritize twelve-step meetings and healthy relationships. We even talked directly about her needing to do things on purpose.

Poets and jazz musicians know this experience well—they're constantly whittling down their art, choosing carefully what is needed for the whole and what isn't. Good art isn't slapdash, no matter how much it may look that way to the untrained eye. There is purpose in every brushstroke and syncopation. A while back, I went to a jazz club with my good friend Jake, an alum of the university's jazz percussion program, to hear one of his heroes play. I asked Jake what made this guy a better drummer than he was, because they were both so good. He said, "He's playing what the music needs."

That ain't easy. Doing something on purpose is no guarantee that it'll work. You'll probably still fail a lot of the time. It's about choosing to work on something regardless of whether it succeeds. It's about being intentional. My husband pokes a lot of fun at me because I'm always exhorting people to be "present and intentional." He wonders if we can arrange the cheese on a plate so it's present and intentional. (We absolutely can.) He asks if we should clean the gutters with presence and intention. (Let's do.) Pick a thing, and you can do it with intention, do it well, for a purpose, with an eye toward the possibilities. We can do things intentionally so that we're engaged with the world and how it turns out. It's a question of asking what's needed.

Early in the life of the Edge House, we had a crisis. One of our students, Walter (not his real name for obvious reasons), disclosed to me that he had a criminal record and was on probation. He told me this through thick plexiglass and a telephone receiver at the downtown jail after he'd violated that probation. What his original offense was and what the violation was are not important, except to say that he was not at all a danger to our campus community. What is important is how our community responded to it.

I could have told him he was no longer welcome with us. Instead, I called together twelve of our most active and thoughtful students. I asked Walter himself, since released from jail, to share information about his offenses and how he was working through the aftermath of them. I asked the students to share their thoughts and feelings about it. And then I asked them to consider what made someone welcome in our community. What do we value about individual humans and about those who had clumped together to form the Edge House? A few of the words we scribbled on a giant sticky note were hospitality and participation, honesty and confidentiality, creativity and discernment, fallibility and noncoercion. From that conversation came our Rule of Life, a short document that describes our community and shapes us at the same time. We read and revise it every year, reminding ourselves of who we say we are. Because we took Walter seriously, because we asked what was needed to care for him and the community, we now have this long-standing tradition of empathy and self-awareness. It's who we are.

You can choose to respond differently than you always have, to move your attention, to experiment and practice. The following is a four-step practice you could try that will not be easy in the slightest. Let's call it the Massively Difficult but Ultimately Rewarding Four-Step Process for Doing Shit on Purpose. The MDURFSPDSP. We'll workshop the name.

The first thing is to ask yourself what you need to be more intentional about, what you can pay more attention to. What parts of the script you've been living with do you want to do more of and what parts do you want to leave behind? Don't tackle all of it at once; just pick one thing to be getting on with.

Second, notice what keeps you from being intentional or what keeps you asleep. A lot of us numb our pain with a drink or three each night or snacks because we're bored. Some of us pick fights with family or friends because it makes us feel in control. We shop or watch Netflix. We avoid the news and convince ourselves that everything is okay or compulsively scroll through social-media newsfeeds. We let our self-hatred take the wheel and assume failure is the end of the story. What stands in the way of seeing the world around you more clearly?

It could be something fairly simple but still immensely difficult to let go of. Just taking your phone out of your pocket, checking the time, and putting it back triggers the same pleasure centers in your brain that drugs and video games do. Folks are shocked when I tell them that at the Edge House, my students and I don't have our phones available to us during important group conversations like discipleship huddles or weekly dinner-church. "How do you make them do that?" they ask. "Don't those young people want to be on the Facebooks or look at dank memes all the time?" I don't make them; I ask them. In the very first year, I asked them to set the phones aside, and they've been doing it ever since. These days, we have a basket everyone puts their phones in to avoid the temptation of sending that one text or looking up that one existential philosopher.

Third, once you've noticed some things that get in your way, create structures that support choosing things rather than being steamrolled by your life. I wanted to pray in the quiet before the pandemonium of getting kids off to school, which meant I had to go to bed by 10:30 p.m., which meant I had to have an alarm at night to get me to stop faffing about: structure. When I was in high school and struggling with my temper, my father suggested I think to myself "In the name of the Father, and the Son, and the Holy Spirit" before I say anything at all. That's one hell of an intention. Maybe it's just a question of writing down your thoughts or saying them out loud that will motivate you to be intentional. Get a journal or find a soul-friend you can marinate on your needs with. Just like having an exercise partner means you're more likely to actually do exercise, having an accountability partner and a structure means you're more likely to do whatever you need to do on purpose.

And last, after you've taken some steps to be more intentional, whether it succeeded or not, celebrate. You can have a full-on house party every time you remember to take out the trash if you want. You can show your partner the little patch of the garden you've weeded and bask in their accolades. The point is you've broken out of the bonds of sleepwalking. You've taken action to change the way things are. You're driving, no matter how good a driver you are, and that choice is cause for celebration.

In conclusion, do shit on purpose, don't let it do you.

# 3

# Sucking at Something Is the First Step to Being Sorta Good at Something*

> Good judgment comes from
> experience. Experience
> comes from bad judgment.
> —My mother. Probably yours, too

A few years ago, a friend of mine brought a conference to town called the Epic Fail Pastors' Conference. They didn't invite inspirational speakers whose churches had grown from twenty

---

*Jake the Dog, *Adventure Time*, season 1, episode 25.

to twenty thousand or whose personal stories of facing over-whelming odds led to triumph with the help of our Lord and Savior Jesus Christ and you can, too! They invited participants to speak together about their failures. They were invited to bring their fear, their botched expectations, their low numbers. They brought their cardboard cut-out, smiley success stories and acknowledged them for what they were: bullshit.

The conference was designed to allow space for folks to tell their stories of failure and not to immediately jump to an after-school-special version of events where everyone learned a Very Special Lesson. They weren't meant to wallow in misery, exactly, but to sit with one another, to affirm the difficulty of ministry and, you know, life. So much of what all of us do meets a stone wall or just trips all over its own feet and spills its books and tampons all over the hallway right in front of its crush. Every one of us struggles to make connections, to be understood, to make headway in the things we love or need. It almost doesn't matter whether the expectations of success were so ridiculously high that failure was inevitable and something to protect our-selves from, or whether the thing was the simplest possible task and we still failed. It hurts. Failure is a constant, solidified by our inevitable deaths.

So these folks talked about failure as a spiritual discipline. The conference sounded amazing. And I failed to go. Because of course.

These kinds of things—small things like missing a confer-ence just as much as big things like failing to dismantle racism in America—make us feel bad, shameful, less than everyone else. I don't know what your stuff is that you bring to the table, but I'd bet a lot of money that you feel like you suck just as much as I do. You've got your own flavor of sucking at things: loneliness, pain, silence, emotional constipation. Personally, I'm never good enough, haven't worked hard enough, haven't fixed enough. I mean, look how broken the world is: clearly I've failed. Me, personally.

The good news is: of course you don't know what you're doing.

Does that not sound like good news? It is, though. None of us know what we're doing, not really. It's all an experiment. And we're not very good at it a lot of the time. But that suckiness, that failure, is not the end. Or, rather, failure is the end of something, but it's not the end of everything. It's part of the process.

Kids are bad at everything at first: tying their shoes, feeding themselves, even holding up their own heads when they're born. Because of course they are, they've never done it before. It's hard as hell and they fuss and cry and when we encourage them to keep experimenting with their muscles and brains, they get it. My daughter crawled with an odd tripod half-crawl, half-crouch gait that, while unconventional, worked for her because she kept at it.

We adults are bad at everything at first as well, but we've got these big brains putting a value judgment on it, calling ourselves stupid or failures, calling other people the same things.

Honestly, adults are just toddlers with larger vocabularies to hide behind. But it doesn't have to be that way.

A few years ago, one of my students at the Edge House left. I call it his walkabout. He'd had a transformative summer as a camp counselor, playing games and teaching skills and being present for the campers' struggles. It was one of those right-place-right-time moments. But leaving something so good and coming back to the regular world is hard. The everyday of life back home can feel like death. Plus, he'd changed his major at the beginning of the summer. He felt good about the decision but also felt the burden of more time in school and the expectations of his parents. And both his siblings had started at our university. He loves them, but he'd made a particular kind of life here. How would they fit into it? What would they bring with them from their childhood relationships that he'd rather leave behind? Then he and one of his good friends ended up in an unrelated conflict, which we worked on mediating, but when he realized the pain he had caused her, it all felt like too much. He needed to take a break. Not from school, from us. So he left.

Something you should know about the community at the Edge House: people don't leave. Not in a creepy, horror-film way; they graduate and everything. But once they find us, we're committed to each other, and they typically stick around. So his clean break was a new thing, and it was like an open wound. It was open-ended as well; we didn't know when he'd come back or even if he would. We agreed to give him space to work out his shit and to reconnect with him at the end of the semester. So far, so good, right?

Wrong. My immediate, visceral, so-powerful-it-must-be-the-truth feeling was that his leaving was a sign that everything I'd done since I'd started six years before was wrong. Everything. Obviously, right? This one beloved student needing to work on his shit away from us means we have failed from the get-go. Lies. A friend of mine says this is the devil at work, not an external force of evil but that little, insidious voice that tells us everything we do is garbage.

His leaving was precisely what we needed as a community, not because he was dreadful, but because we needed to learn how to let someone leave and how to trust them to do their own work. We needed to identify and separate our own emotional stuff from his. As painful as it was, it was good practice. He came back to us the next semester more grounded, more aware of himself, and now we can't get rid of him. He doesn't shy away from conflict and has helped other students feel their feelings and ask for what they need. He has been a huge positive influence on so many people's lives.

The life of this community is a process, not a product. What we felt in that moment as sucking at friendship and conversation was part of a larger story we couldn't yet see. Because of it, now we're kinda good at friendship and conversation.

My mother taught me to sew as I was growing up and, spoilers, I can make real-ass clothing now, but back then, it was rough. She'd show me something simple, and I'd think, "Sure,

I got this." I did not got this. I'd lose control and stitch places I shouldn't. I'd break needles because I didn't take out the metal pins holding the fabric together. Something would catch and then suddenly the machine would groan and make a huge tangled mess on the back of the fabric and I would scream and cry angry tears and hit the machine and hurt my hand and feel miserable because there was no way ever I could do this right. Ever. (Once, even longer ago, I was trying to learn embroidery and stitched my project to the pajamas I was wearing at the time.) Anyway, there were a lot of false starts. And my mother's advice when I brought her something that wasn't stitched right was, "Rip it out." Ugh. What a failure. I mean, yeah, it's just a dress seam, but having to rip out my work and do it again felt like there was something wrong with me. Why did I suck so badly at this? If I'd stopped there at the moment of suck, it would have been the end. But dutifully, resentfully, I went back and ripped out the seam to stitch it again. And again and again sometimes. But after years of this, slowly, each time, I got sort of good at it. And then pretty good at it. And eventually, pretty damned good.

Something stands in our way of opening ourselves up to failure as part of a process. I think it's that we humans spend a lot of energy on a binary between success and failure that doesn't exist. It's not that those concepts don't exist, but that the binary itself doesn't. It's that old saw about trying not to see in black and white. We think if we've succeeded at all, we can't be failures, and if we fail, whatever that means, we can't possibly be successful. But that's so static, so unhelpful, and not even a good description of what's really happening. It's not that success or progress or winning doesn't exist, it's that they're lies. And it's not that failure or decline or losing doesn't exist, it's that they're lies as well. They're all lies we tell ourselves because life's not actually a competition. Any win or loss is only temporary. My theater history professor said the only difference between comedy and tragedy is when you end the story: comedies end with marriage or some sort of achievement. Tragedies end with death. Just lots and lots of death. The point being, if you stop telling the story at the wedding or a joke or socioeconomic success, it's all good, everyone's happy. But if you keep telling that story, you'll get to the couple's first argument or the death of a parent or a weird national election, and suddenly you're in a tragedy where failure is ever-present. And then if you keep telling the story, the couple works out their issues with the help of a counselor or good friend, they move through their grief, or another election happens and someone else is in charge.

Now, I need to take a step back for a moment to say that there are real failures in this world: our failure as a country to recognize the HIV/AIDS epidemic for what it was; Syria's and Myanmar's failures to treat their "threatening minorities," their citizens, as human beings; Christianity's superhuman ability over twenty centuries to misunderstand Jesus's life as justification for more violence against outsiders. It's not a question about whether something is good or bad; it's what we do with the whole ball of wax. To put it another way, there are Very Bad Things we humans do that might have been considered success or failure in their moment, even though history views them differently now. Looking back, it might seem that we don't learn anything from our past failures, our past cruelties, but we do. Sometimes we learn how to be more efficient in our cruelties, and sometimes we learn to hear the cry of the victim. We learn—very slowly—how to resolve conflict with less violence. Not no violence—that's a long, long way off—but less. We have failed spectacularly to treat other humans well, and even these failures offer the possibility of learning something. The question is, what do we do once we see them? Not to trivialize any tragedies we experience, but even these offer the possibility of a process.

Neither success nor failure is permanent. They both offer the possibility of learning something, and they both can disappear in the blink of an eye. In a way, what I'm talking about is a kind of amalgam of success and failure that I'll call *successandfailure*. Rolls trippingly off the tongue, no? If you think about success and failure as isolated, physical objects on a spectrum—success over here on the left, a bright and shiny brass ring, and failure over here on the right, a stinky pile of garbage that makes you uncomfortable to look at—then you can start to see the space between them as having some value as well. A critically acclaimed performance or presentation where you felt nauseated the whole time might be in that space, a kind of successandfailure. A day when you felt so weighed down by your depression that all you could do was get up to brush your teeth and then go back to bed, another kind of successandfailure.

In other words, you're looking not at the ends of the spectrum but at the whole spectrum itself as a process. The entire thing, including the space between, is valuable. It's the difference between feeling how fast a car is going while you're inside it and sitting alongside the road and seeing that car change speeds. If you dig math, it's like success and failure are the first derivative and successandfailure is the second derivative. Or if you dig art, it's like success and failure are in constant motion, constantly showing you different angles of their surface, constantly changing hue like those surprisingly soothing videos of someone mixing paint with a palette knife. Iridescent white and dark purple and turquoise and a touch of flat, rusty orange. The palette knife begins mixing, and first you've still got the separate colors in ribbons. Then they start blending and making something beautifully unexpected and then something entirely new.

Think about it this way: in the scientific community, not knowing something is what makes you a good scientist. It means you're able to ask questions about what you don't know. We read an article at the Edge House called "The Importance of Stupidity in Scientific Research." It's not an anti-science screed but the experience of a scientist who, stumped about something he was working on, went for help to his experts-in-their-fields mentors, and they didn't have the answers. He realized that *of course* no one had the answers to his questions, that was the whole point of doing the research and experiments in the first place. He writes, "The crucial lesson was that the scope of things I didn't know wasn't merely vast; it was, for all practical purposes, infinite. That realization, instead of being discouraging, was liberating. If our ignorance is infinite, the only possible course of action is to muddle through as best we can." [3]

Even as we muddle through, there's the recognition that something has changed, there's something new happening. Successandfailure means experimentation rather than competition, and that can be uncomfortable. Trying to do that new thing, whether it's learning new information or trying out a new physical skill or allowing ourselves to feel a particular feeling we don't like, is terrible at the beginning. We want to run away and call the experiment a failure and ourselves failures as well because we haven't practiced it. My five-year-old son was so concerned before going into kindergarten that he didn't already know the things they would learn that year. And in kindergarten he was worried about first grade. He stewed on it in the car and in a quavery voice asked, "Will they help me if I don't know how to do it?" (He's doing great, by the way.) Not already knowing the answers is scary, yes. But consider this: not having to already know something makes it so much easier to experiment—the possible options are suddenly unlimited.

What I love about failure as part of a process instead of an end point is how freeing it is. In a competition model, there are too many restrictions on the possibilities. A conversation becomes something you can win. A relationship becomes something you can win. Love and freedom and sobriety become things you can win. In a process model, we're always growing and changing rather than racing for one completed, perfect moment. When we experiment, we are ready to see something new and, because of that, we are much freer.

One way to experiment with your own sense of failure is to talk about it with someone else. I know, that sounds like the worst, but it will help. Most of us vent about how unfair the world is to us, but while it's important work to release our feelings, that's not what this is. Ask someone you trust to explore an example of failure in your life with you and to ask questions about it. What's a different way to look at it? Even if it feels too shiny-happy, how can you reframe it to be about possibilities? What can you learn?

A couple of years ago, we had a lovely new student named Zachary. He dove right into the community, washing dishes after dinner-church, being vulnerable in his discipleship group, playing board games at the drop of a hat. He was thoughtful and compassionate. He just slotted right in to our communal life. Partway through the semester, he shared something with me that caused him deep shame. The specifics are not something I will share here, but I was uncertain whether I was required to report them to a higher authority and deeply conflicted about whether I thought I should. I said all this out loud. In the midst of a tender, honest conversation, I tried to navigate between support and clarity about my responsibility. He was devastated, obviously. As it turns out, I was not required to report, but the damage had been done. Zachary wanted nothing to do with me or the community because of what he experienced as a betrayal. It crushed me. As I imagine it crushed him as well. I was doing the best I could with the information I had, and I could not have failed in a worse fashion. He is doing well, out there in the world, and I have learned to be more circumspect and to consult before speaking. In the aftermath, we've both found a place of successandfailure, which is good news, even though it doesn't always feel that way.

We are all moving from one place to another—emotionally, spiritually, physically. It takes a hell of a lot of time and a courage to see failure not as the end but as a possibility. You don't win life; you live it.

# 4

# Take Off the Costume

By the 6th grade I stopped doing ordinary things in front of people. It had been ordinary to sing, kids are singing all the time when they are little, but then something happens. It's not that we stop singing. I still sang. I just made sure I was alone when I did it and I made sure I never did it accidentally. That thing we call "bursting into song." I believe this happens to most of us. We are still singing, but secretly and all alone.
—Lynda Barry, *What It Is*

When my friends and I are waiting around at comics or gaming conventions, one of our pastimes is to play a game we call "Costume or Clothes?" The idea is, while people-watching, to guess whether what the person is wearing is a costume—whether or not it's a recognizable character—or clothing. It's harder than you'd think. That person over there next to the coffee kiosk is clearly someone damn creepy from a video game I don't play, and that other dude is definitely dressed in the best Supergirl cosplay I've ever seen. That chick is wearing a Wonder Woman shirt and a steampunk-y skirt, but I'm pretty sure it's clothes. And that guy over there—is he dressed as *Where's Waldo*? Or is he just wearing a striped shirt? To be clear, it's not a game of mockery, but one of discernment and fascination. What are folks communicating with what they're wearing?

I wear a costume all the time. It's a black dress shirt, short-sleeved, with a special placket in the front that hides the buttons for some reason. It's got a smooth white collar that goes all the way around my neck and attaches with these little metal studs that I'm constantly losing. It's got jeans in various states of disrepair, Chuck Taylors or funky boots, a comfy sweater, but it's the black shirt and white collar that are consistent and consistently communicating. It says, "I'm a priest!" I like to think it says, "I'm approachable!" I'm sure it says to some people, "Danger! Christian! Run away!" When I'm feeling snarky, I hope it says, "I'm not like one of *those* Christians." Regardless of what I want it to say and how other people see it, it's a costume.

A costume is the visual result of the choices we make about how to be seen. Actors wear them, of course, and the colors and styles communicate all kinds of things to the audience, like the characters' time period, relative wealth, emotional or psychological state, connections with other characters. Drag queens and street performers and clergy wear them. Musicians in the orchestra wear them to present a uniform, formal look. Even members of the military are wearing a kind of costume, the medals and stripes and fabrics all communicating something about rank and tenure and location. Just so with our day-to-day clothing. What you choose to put on each day, whether you're aware of it or not, signals something to people who see you. So, you can make a case that our "Costume or Clothes" game is kind of pointless since it's all a costume.

The key word in my definition above is *choices*: casual or formal, hot or cold, professional or sexy, comforting or provocative, and some intersection of all of this. We wear things we like. We wear things that make us look good. Or fierce. Or vulnerable. We choose something physical to project something metaphysical. And sometimes there is no choice, which itself communicates something. We wear things we have to wear because it's a uniform or it's all that's clean or it's all we've got. I just saw a photo of a four-year-old boy who'd walked with a group of refugees across a desert in Syria to find safety with only the clothes on his back and a small plastic bag with two pieces of clothing in it: one from his mother and one from his sister. Four years old. Light as his bag was, I wondered what he thought about this flight from home and how inconceivable it was that this little human could carry such a weight with him as he fled. The clothing he took and wore tells us about what matters to him and how desperate his situation is.

I spend a lot of time in the theater department on our university campus. I do office hours there, which means every week I walk down into the basement of the performing arts building and hang out in a semi-enclosed public area known as the Fishbowl. It's got a huge corkboard on one wall, table and chairs, and a glass-block wall that curves around two sides of it. Sometimes I'm alone and get a lot of work done on the computer; sometimes students and faculty seek me out to talk.

This may seem obvious, but actors aren't the only people involved in staging a play. For it to work, you need all kinds of people who rely on each other. The actors have to trust the techs to build sets and rigging that will look good and keep them safe. The techs have to trust each other with dangerous tools and each other's aesthetic choices, and they trust the actors with the enacting of what they've been creating. It all works together.

And in the theater, everything is a choice: what color to paint the set or when to pick up a prop or what shoes the character wears. Even nakedness is a choice and can be a way not only to communicate but also to hide. In the BBC show *Sherlock*, the character Irene Adler presents herself in the nude when she first shows up to meet Sherlock Holmes. Because she isn't wearing clothes, he has very little information to deduce anything about her. Her nudity, while seemingly vulnerable, is a smokescreen to hide her intentions, another costume. Physical nakedness can make us uncomfortable because we assume sensuality but also because it confronts us with how defenseless we really are. Our skin is easily bruised, our bones easily broken, our life so easily taken. So we use our literal clothes—or sets or costumes—to hide our feelings and desires.

Our personalities are also a form of costume, communicating a little of ourselves and hiding even more. Extroversion and anger for justice are the costume I wear to communicate confidence and safety. Inside I'm a hot, crazy, truck-fire mess of a person who disappoints important people. And that description right there is another costume: I don't really think I'm that awful inside, but I put it on so that you'll be gentler with me or tell me I'm cool and fine. Both of which are true. What I really am—as far as I can tell this particular morning when I'm writing this—is pretty good at what I do, caring for and sometimes grumpy toward people I know well, expansively compassionate for people I don't, and also deeply judgmental toward people I think should know better. I am, as Martin Luther called us all, simultaneously a saint and a sinner.

I had a student several years ago who, in his words, was a pathological liar. I think he used that label to hide, a harsh judgment used to protect himself from other people's judgment. Nevertheless, he did lie a bit. And like a lot of us, it was a defense mechanism. He told us at first that he'd been a pot dealer and was a kind of street tough working on changing his ways. He's a physically big dude and has a bit of an intimidating air, so we took that at face value. As our relationship progressed, we saw more and more clearly his soft, chewy center. He was a sweet, caring man who was afraid of being hurt, so projected this huge, hard-candy exterior.

One morning, he borrowed my car to pick up milk for our espresso giveaway that day. He returned, we continued preparations, we chatted easily. After about ten minutes, he casually said, "When I left, I noticed some scratches on the side of your car. They've been there a while, right?" I said, "Yup, that car tends to get a little banged up, it's no big deal." After a few more minutes, he asked, "How many scratches would you say were on there?" I paused and looked him in the eye. "I don't know, a few, back right side near the wheel. Maybe a few farther up on the side. Why?" He said, "Just wondering." You and I both know something else was coming. I waited. He eventually said, like it would be a surprise, "So, I didn't want to say anything, but getting out of the parking lot was a little tight around the corner, and I think I scraped your car a little." "I know," I said, and we went out to look at it together. There were indeed new scratches, but I was much less concerned for the car and more impressed with him slowly peeling back emotional layers to expose the worry about what he'd done. This was one of the first moments he let me see his vulnerable self underneath the costume of being in control. Once he realized it was allowed, he worked hard on letting himself be seen for the four years he was with us.

We talk at the Edge House about how everyone has a wound: a deeply held, spiritual wound from when they discovered the world doesn't love them unconditionally. Everyone's wound is different, of course, has a different kind of pain and resonance. This isn't some form of "poor little snowflake" bullshit—every single person in this world is hurt because the world is hard. Your wound might have been from a particular, traumatic moment in childhood, or maybe it was a slow burn. Maybe you can't even articulate what exactly it is, but we all have it, and we all protect that wound with metaphorical layers of bandage. We don't want anyone to touch it because, dammit, it hurts. And sometimes we get so good at protecting the hurt, we build up so many layers of personality, so many layers of defense mechanism, that we don't even see the wound ourselves. This protection is what I'm talking about with the costume metaphor. If we truly want to be known, if we truly want to change the habits and patterns we carve out every day, we have to take off the costumes we're wearing. Peeling back the layers we've built up to protect our heartsickness is painful in itself. It makes us vulnerable to other people. If you see even a hint of what makes me sad, you could hurt me more. And yet the only way out of this pain is through it. The only way out is to get nekkid.

On a broad scale, our country is wrapped up in the layers of self-protection we've built around ourselves. We say we're the greatest, most exceptional country (or we've got to get back to that mythical time when we were). We think racism is over because we had a black president, or we think anyone who criticizes social-justice efforts is automatically a bigot. We think sexual assault is uncommon and perpetrated by obvious creeps we can avoid easily, and anyway, false rape accusations are just as common. We think our own actions have no effect on the climate, that straight, white men are the worst thing since sliced bread, that pointing out someone's hypocrisy is both righteous and effective.

We are beginning to see that these things all hide wounds. We have never looked hard and clear as a country at the massacre that was slavery or ever made amends to the people whose families and lives were ripped apart. This is a festering wound in the body of our civic life, poisoning everything it touches. We have plenty of food on this planet to feed every single person well, yet Americans starve when they can't afford it and are sold junk food on every corner. A current Christian heresy called *prosperity gospel* makes us think that when we have it good, it's because we deserve it, and when we have it bad, we deserve that, too. These things cut us to pieces, leave us bleeding on the floor. But we cover it up with a bandage and limp away.

As a country, we are starting to wake up to how things have not changed as much as we thought, how the wounds we carry as a people have not healed over but are still very tender to the touch. Waking up leaves us flayed open. And it's because some of our costume has slipped. It's scary, and it feels like loss. The nakedness we feel when we look at white supremacist marches in Charlottesville or the pain inherent in the #MeToo movement or the determination in the eyes of high-school students from Parkland, Florida, is deeply uncomfortable. It leaves us vulnerable. But not nearly as vulnerable as our black brothers and sisters, as the children separated from their families at the border, as queer youth in their schools and on the street. We who haven't felt physically vulnerable—or who haven't felt this particular vulnerability—are starting to see the pain around us. We are starting to see the protective costume we've been wearing that says It's All Fine across the chest. It's not fine.

That uncomfortable, vulnerable feeling can be a gift as well as a loss. It can push us into action out in the world and also into seeing things differently. The first step is seeing that you're even wearing a costume. Ask yourself what patterns you fall into when you're stressed, how you protect yourself when someone yells at you or when you're anxious. Even what clothes you wear when you need to project confidence or softness or trustworthiness. I've noticed over the years that when I'm nervous about confronting someone about bad behavior, I start talking to myself about minutiae I see around me. "Man, need to make sure we do laundry today. What's that weird smell? Oh, yeah, don't forget to order more espresso beans." I hide behind busywork. I am afraid of how the other person will react to what I have to say, so I make myself look nonthreatening while also being in charge. It's a pattern, and seeing it that way, noticing not just once but over time, is necessary for change.

The next step, I think, is to gently look at whatever pattern or costume you're seeing without defensiveness. You aren't a bad person for doing this thing. You're simply protecting a deeper pain. Imagine this costume or pattern physically in front of you—maybe in your cupped hands—and look at it or yourself with kindness, like the way many parents look when their kids give them macaroni art. At the very least, look at it neutrally— that is, hold this costume you wear and look at it without calling it ugly or stupid. Be curious about what it protects. What is the pain that this costume soothes or helps you ignore? This may take some time, and that's fine.

Just doing this much may open you up in ways you couldn't have imagined before. This kind of self-examination, which on the surface seems simple, is some of the hardest work humans can do. It's no wonder most of us don't do it. But gentle self-observation can be like the first day after you've been really sick: the whole world had been shrunk down to your nausea or congestion or exhaustion, surviving was the only thing that mattered. When it's gone, the world is vast and full of possibilities, the sun is shining brighter, and life is worth living again.

For extra credit, try imagining someone else in your life undertaking this same process, holding themselves gently, seeing their own pain and defense mechanisms clearly. Imagine holding that person in your cupped palms and looking at them with kindness. Every single person around you has an inner wound, protects their wound with layers and layers of stories about themselves, and wrestles with really letting anyone in. Yes, even that one guy.

When we have protesters or preachers on campus, both they and the people who show up to challenge them are wearing a kind of costume. They've hidden their real selves. They aren't really hearing each other; they aren't seeing each other as real people but as representatives of larger, threatening ideologies. What might it be like if a student from Turning Point, a conservative campus activist group, and a student from our women and gender studies department sat down over coffee to be vulnerable with their doubts and joys instead of trying to win the conversation?

The best part of taking off your costume, the absolute best part, is truly being known. There's no more hiding, no more fear. Letting yourself be seen by the people you love then gives them permission to let themselves be seen as well. You can both give and receive love more easily. I sat down recently with a woman in my congregation who hasn't cared much for me over the last nine years. I said to her, "I'm not everyone's cup of tea, but I did notice that you seemed not to like me. What's changed?" Her response was apologetic and honest and maybe a tad self-protective (who wouldn't be?), but that one conversation over coffee and avocado toast cleansed the space between us that had become a kind of wound. Though we haven't arrived at our final relational destination, we each let the other see some of our insecurities and more of our deeper selves. We left that conversation smiling and hugging. Change is entirely possible.

Whatever your costume is—The Most Competent Person in the Room, or Unnecessarily Apologetic in Uncontentious Situations, or Small and Quiet Person Who Goes Unnoticed, or Average American Who Just Wants a Beer—it's only a part of who you are. Whatever it is inside you that hurts can't be healed until you peel back the layers protecting it.

Take it off. Take it all off.

# 5

# If It's Not Okay, It's Not the End

> I am glad you are here with me.
> Here at the end of all things, Sam.
> —Frodo Baggins, *The
> Return of the King*

Everything dies. Were you hoping for an uplifting chapter? Have patience, we'll get there, but new life only happens to dead things, so we need to start here.

You know already that death is all around: school shootings, epidemics, suicides, hurricanes and earthquakes, conflicts over land or religion or pipeline building, celebrities, family members. It's no wonder some Christians mistakenly think the

Bible prophesied these as the Last Days. (They aren't, and anyway, that's not what the prophets were doing in the first place. But that's another book.) Even though the fact of death is ever-present and threatening, we humans have excelled at coming up with ways to forget about it. We build buildings and cities. We make art and do science. We make love and war, and every one of these things is an attempt to push our deaths back, to pretend and not think on it. Even art specifically about death is a way to keep the artist alive. Even war is busywork to maintain the living borders of a nation.

And we sure as hell don't want to explain death to our children, our beautiful children who should be so far from death as to make it impossible, our children who fill up pediatric cancer wards or are ripped from our arms at the border or who are lost to human trafficking. I can talk to my own kids about sex any time—the sex talk is easy—but death? How do I explain that people don't last forever, that the world around them will eventually die, that they will experience hurts and betrayals all their lives that feel like death? My kids get upset that the flowers they picked shriveled or their helium balloons shrank and sank to the floor. How do I tell them that their father and I will one day not be around without breaking down in tears and making it even worse? The way I've gone about it is to say about the flowers and balloons and favorite restaurants that close, "I'm so sorry, these things don't last forever." I've said it enough times that when Abi was five and our hairdresser died, she said, "Like flowers and balloons."

The story Christians and Jews tell about the beginning of all things is also a story about the end of all things—many people see it as a morality tale about the origin of sin, but I read it as a plot twist early in the story, as the sudden awareness that we are able to die. The story goes that we humans lived in a beautiful garden that was everything to us and that would always be our home. It was so much everything and always that we couldn't imagine anything else. Then we ate the fruit of the knowledge of good and evil, and we saw clearly that it could end. Good things, bad things, small things, huge things—they all end eventually. And that is flagrantly not okay.

On a college campus, death is surprisingly present. Our campus is currently enrolled at something like forty-six thousand students plus faculty and staff. With a population that large, we have dozens of people die each year—some suicide, some disease, some accidents. It's always sobering to receive the "dear colleague" email giving the name and details of the most recent death and even more so to attend the annual memorial service commemorating all the students and staff who have died that year. Part of the Episcopal burial service says, "In the midst of life, we are in death."

There are a lot of endings that feel like death. Divorce, according to a good friend of mine, felt like their marriage had been a living thing and had died. The church changing and shifting in this new millennium seems like death to older generations who feel that change as surely as they begin to feel their own mortality. Rejection by a lover, the loss of an election, or simply being ill can feel like death warmed-over. We humans generally don't do well with endings because they're frightening and awkward. We regularly say, "It's not goodbye," to avoid calling something the end. What if no one else wants to talk to me or be my friend? What if this new thing falls apart? What if, when I leave, no one cares about the thing I care about and keeps it going?

Every time someone leaves our campus ministry, it feels like a death. Whether a student leaves because of a move, because of graduation, or because they need something different than what we offer, the community changes irrevocably. At the university I serve, we have an intense co-op program where students alternate taking classes one semester with working in their field of study the next, so our community changes every semester. They're here and then they're not. In a way, we are set up for planned obsolescence: we teach them awareness and empathy and healthy relationships and then send them out into the world. It's terrifying in the run up to the first weeks of class in the fall because we have no idea what new people will show up or how they will change the community when they do. I'm not being hyperbolic when I say, in late August, my inner Alice is constantly jumping up and down and yelling "Will anyone love us again?"

A friend once told me campus ministry is like farming. The fall is your planting season: you get excited about all the beans and squash and rhubarb and potatoes you're putting in and what all you can cook with them. On campus, it's getting out there and meeting people, being seen, inviting folks in, and establishing rhythms with the regular folks. The winter is your growing season: you start to notice that the potatoes aren't doing as well as you'd hoped, and for some reason, the beans have done diddly-squat. So you revise your expectations and go with the fruit you're likely to have, the squash and rhubarb. On campus that means the people who show up are the people who need to be there. It means you let some events die because no one's interested. The spring is your harvest season: the piles and piles of squash and rhubarb are delightful, and you've got a handful of potatoes in there as well. Harvest season is also when all the plants die back. It's the season of celebration with the people who've engaged with the community and a season of saying goodbye. Harvest is what you've been building to as a farmer, and it's both a relief and a sadness. The summer is your fallow season: you let the land and yourself rest and grieve while you plan again for the fall.

It's a cycle of life and death, restarting the ministry every year. Campus ministry goes through all the same things churches or other organizations do, only in a much-compressed timeline. Your business or family or kayak club goes through the same cycle, and at some point you or someone else resists the season of death. Because of course you do. We don't want good things to end, even if the good thing was decades ago. And even bad things can become so familiar that we fear their ending even as we long for things to be better. Every damn year at the Edge House, graduation is wonderful and heart-wrenching. Endings are real. They're always present. And at the same time, they're not the end of the story.

Remember when Superman died back in the nineties and people breathlessly talked about it on the national news? Or more recently when Captain America was a Nazi and fans wrote strongly worded tweets? Nothing will ever be the same, they said, there's no coming back from this. Even though this sort of thing had happened many times before and there was indeed a coming back from it. It's disingenuous because those moments sell comics, but they don't last. They never do.

There's a line sometimes attributed to Brazilian poet Fernando Sabino: "Everything will be okay in the end. If it's not okay, it's not the end." I saw it the first time on a greeting card, of all places, and ended up getting it tattooed on my bicep. Death, endings, and general not-okay-ness are none of them really the end. When I hit my head on the tailgate of my car when I'm loading groceries, it hurts like hell and I'm spittin' mad. But the pain and embarrassment subside, and I learn again that there are hard objects in this world and I am clumsy.

Sabino takes as a point of faith that eventually everything will be okay—the universe will bend toward justice, emptiness will be filled, violence will decline. The when is not specified, nor is the manner in which things will be okay. But, at some point, maybe sooner than you think, it will be. In the meantime—when things are not okay because it's not over—there's still the possibility of a comedy instead of a tragedy, there's still a choice available. It's not necessarily a good choice, one you want to make, but it's there. Not-okay-ness means something can change.

You may be reading this from an atheist or agnostic per-spective, and I respect your objection that death itself is a pretty firm ending. I led an interfaith vigil after the Pulse nightclub massacre in 2016, and in my remarks I used Sabino's words. A friend of mine later told me that as I said, "If it's not okay, it's not the end," a man in the crowd near him whispered to him-self, pained, "Not for them." My heart broke all over again. I'm not trying to get you to believe like I do—that's not the point of this book or of Christianity. I only want to share the hope I feel when I look at the vastness of the universe. What we don't know and how much we don't know is fascinating. Plants and oceans and stars and the fabric of the universe are constantly and mysteriously renewing themselves. There's always the potential for more knowledge, more connections among the things we already understand. That it is not yet the end, to me, is a kind of reassurance.

Elizah came to us several years ago with almost nothing. She was sleeping in her car and struggling to get to her classes each day. She was a capable, loving young woman who'd hit a rough patch and didn't know how to get out of it. Her school loans, while not enormous by many standards, were more than she could pay, and when her car was impounded because she parked too long, she felt lost. Her life felt like it was at a dead end, cornered by wild dogs or something. It was very much not okay. She and I had a lot of conversations about her responses to stress—freezing like a deer in headlights, mostly—and I often reminded her that she could ask for what she needed. She didn't have to struggle along alone. She moved into my spare bedroom for a few months, so she could work and save money for a place of her own. Because of her willingness to try something new and the Edge House community's willingness to invite her in, her story didn't end there. She's back in school, has her own apartment, is working on paying down her loans, and is helping another student learn to cook. She has friends, a community, and maybe more importantly, an awareness that her life is filled with possibility. What had seemed like the beginning of the end transformed into a beginning, full stop.

And there are times when a real, proper ending is a good thing. When I worked as a hospital chaplain, there were two old men in the ICU who were dying. One of them had two daughters who kept him listed as a full code, so when his heart or breathing stopped, the nurses had to do everything possible to resuscitate him. This man was in his nineties and barely clinging to life. His daughters could not see past their own need for him to be alive. They couldn't see his life well-lived and his death as a good ending. He hung on for months in the space between life and death. The family of the other man saw their father's death approaching and made their peace with it. They all squeezed into the room, careful of the tubes and wires sprouting from him like vines. I stood there with them, holding his granddaughter's hand, and listened as they said goodbye. His two daughters leaned over him and said, "It's alright, Daddy, it's time to go. We love you." He died during the night. It was almost as though he needed to hear them release him. A good death, a good ending, is a gift.

It's counterintuitive, thinking of death as a gift. It isn't always a gift, that's for damn sure. Visions of bodies floating down the river after Hiroshima or of a man dying on the streets, alone and unmourned come unbidden to mind. But sometimes, sometimes it is. One of our students spent months watching her grandmother suffer from liver disease, and when she died, the student and her family felt relief and gratitude. She wrote to me: "At the very end, it was a gift. She was tired and in pain and the rest of us were tired and sad. . . . Death has never been the worst thing that can happen." And in one of the worst hells humans have created on this earth, Buchenwald concentration camp, a prisoner wrote on a scrap of paper, "Peace to all men of evil will. . . . May we remain in your enemies' memory not as their victims . . . not as haunting spectres, but as helpers in their striving to destroy the fury of their criminal passions."[4] This man, whose experience and probable death there could have been nothing but suffering, offered up his own death as something transformative. There's new life possible, always, in the strangest places.

I used to do preschool chapel with a room full of two- and three-year-olds who always wanted to pray for Spider-Man and dolphins. My favorite story we told was about Good Friday and Easter. We had a set of eight small wood panels painted purple on one side and laminated with simple images of Jesus's life on the other. The stories of Jesus's death and resurrection were laminated onto the same board, one on each side. The schtick was to pass it around and ask them to try to separate the images. Of course they couldn't; it was wood, and they were little. Give me some protective gear and a saw . . . The point was that life and death are inseparable. Jesus's death is meaningless, just another death among millions, if we don't have the story of the resurrection. And the resurrection can't happen at all if he doesn't die first. Trees fall to the forest floor and decompose, enriching the soil for the next generation of trees to grow. Life and death inexorably tied together.

Death is deeply not okay. And simultaneously, it's not the end of the story. When everything feels temporary or tenuous, don't panic. Think of the events of your life like waves coming into the shore—they ebb and flow. Sometimes you feel like you're experiencing a ridiculously long high tide and are up to your neck, but the tide will go out, it always does. Or think of the painful moments of your life as hunger pangs or labor pains—they signify that something else is happening. You might ask yourself what you need to make something okay again. Or, if you're up for a real challenge, what you need so that you'll be okay with the situation, regardless of whether it changes. Is it the situation or your attitude that needs experimentation? I don't know what it is you struggle with, what deaths or endings you're mourning, but I know they're painful. Things are not okay for you. And it's not the end.

Everything dies. It's hard, but it's not the only thing, and it's not the end. Endings are not about goodness or badness, they just are. Death isn't always bad, and life is sure as hell not always good. It ain't over 'til it's okay.

# 6

# It's Okay to Feel Your Feelings

> Write hard and clear about
> what hurts. Don't avoid it. It has
> all the energy. Don't worry, no
> one ever died of it. You might
> cry or laugh, but not die.
> —attributed to Ernest Hemingway

I've got a wheel of emotions image on my phone lock screen because I'm shit at knowing what I'm feeling at any given moment and I need an infographic to articulate it for me. The wheel of emotions is a giant circle with a multitude of nuanced words for different feelings divided into categories, words like *distant, amazed, disillusioned, eager,* and *suspicious.* As a person formally trained in theater and English, you'd think that I could come up with the right words to name what I'm feeling. Mostly what I've got is angry, happy, or sad. I suppose that's pretty good considering my nine-year-old daughter has some titanic-sized feelings and can only say "I don't know" when we ask her about them. But I want and need better ways to express how I'm feeling. I hear you can feel resentful, inadequate, or playful. Who knew? Perhaps, like my loving husband, you're baffled by my lack of self-knowledge. "How could you not know what you're feeling?" he asks, genuinely bewildered.

I'm only joking a little when I say it's recent that I discovered I have feelings at all. I've thought of myself as entirely rational and organized for so long. Critical thinking is a blessing, a delight, something I once lorded over my junior-high-school peers. Any feelings I had weren't feelings so much as unbiased truth that other people couldn't see. Watching my husband and other people struggle through their feelings, I felt a certain superiority. Friends, if you would only think through the process, think through what you're feeling, you'll find, I'm sure, that you needn't feel it at all. How freeing to be so cerebral, do give it a try. Chortle, chortle.

At the same time, I knew I had feelings. I'm not a robot. When Chad (his real name) didn't ask me to a junior-high dance, I sobbed for an hour. When my bosses over the years asked me questions I couldn't answer, I felt small and inadequate. When I preach a sermon that makes even one of my parishioners feel angry or judged, I am, without fail, surprised, wretched, and inconsolable. When my feelings really come out, it's embarrassing, irrational, shameful. Feeling my feelings is perplexing and bad.

Let's recap: I don't know what the hell emotions are, I don't have them, and when I do have them, they're bad. All caught up? To deal with this state of affairs, I pretend that everything's fine, just fine. I've gotten so good at convincing myself everything's fine that when things are not fine, I get angry. Like really angry. I feel my skin prickle and my heart beat faster; I let out a percussive groan or well-placed "dammit." It's like I've got a volcano churning in my gut and when things aren't the way I want them to be, it explodes and burns me and everyone around me. I yell. I have it on good authority that even when I'm silent, my angry face is terrifying. What's sad is I've been angry for much of my life—it's my go-to feeling. Countless times, people have asked me, "Why are you so angry?" "I'm not angry," I'd say angrily, and I'd believe every word.

Slowly, I learned to name this anger, but even describing it here or out loud in the middle of a fraught conversation makes me sound like an ill-mannered toddler who hasn't gotten her way. But that's exactly how I feel sometimes, and I'd be willing to bet most of you do, too. We've just gotten good at hiding our anger behind a veneer of respectability. When I do let myself experience my anger and take the time to examine a little deeper, under the hard-candy shell of anger, I discover a chewy center of sadness. I'm angry a lot because I'm profoundly sad a lot and it's painful, so I'd rather be pissed about it than feel it. I'm so sad and hurt at the pain of the entire world that I add to the pain by lashing out. Which in turn makes me sad again. I feel sadness and anger, then I feel sadness and anger that I'm feeling sadness and anger. It's all very meta.

I'm certain I'm not the only one with a complicated relationship with my feelings. As far as I can tell, our culture here in America is interested either in over-the-top feelings that brew up conflict for entertainment or in not showing emotions at all. The first is the basis of all "reality" television (I put it in quotes because it's some of the most unreal narrative out there) and of our daily interactions about who said what to whom (oh, she did not, you know I can't let that stand). The second is the basis of our efficient and rational professional world where feelings are immaterial to good customer service or writing contracts. The church, interestingly, falls in both camps, simultaneously encouraging big outward shows of emotion and discouraging the real, difficult ones. Neither path acknowledges what's actually going on inside us. Both paths manufacture a false reality. We often prefer these false realities because our real feelings are so messy we don't know how to respond to them and so tender they need to be protected.

Imogen, one of my students at the Edge House, feels all her feelings all the time. It's not drama; they're so present, they overwhelm her. She might come into the Edge House one day infectiously delighted with a joke or the weather or a painting she was working on, her face lit up with joy and her voice bubbling. Or she might come in another day unable to see beyond the futility and fear she holds close to her heart like a locket containing a lover's photo. She doesn't just have feelings; she is her feelings. She isn't feeling them so much as being flattened by them.

Another student, Quinn, struggles with the opposite side of this coin—he's super rational, very focused on teasing out all the nuance of words and concepts. He feels connected with people when he can talk deeply with them about psychology and neuroscience and gender politics. He becomes depressed and withdrawn when people aren't as interested in what he's passionate about, when he worries about what he's supposed to do with his life, or about whether he feels things at all. But Quinn is a deeply compassionate and silly person. His genuine smile is a gift. In actuality, he has so many feelings, he's just been trained to believe they're at best unscientific and useless, so now he doesn't notice them at all.

What both of these students are feeling is real, not something they made up, but it's irrational. That's literally true, because we're not meant to think feelings; we're meant to feel them. Irrationality is really a neutral term, the state of being without reason or logic, the category of things that aren't thoughts. Our feelings give us information our rational selves can't see. It's not a bug, it's a feature. Sometimes there is a logical flow to our feelings—someone insults us, and we feel hurt—and yet we still feel them; the logic doesn't erase them. The only way out of the feeling is through it. In reality, feelings come and go.

They can overwhelm for a time and then dissipate like the wind, leaving us wondering why we felt so strongly to begin with.

We also think feelings are irrelevant—it doesn't matter how we feel about certain things, we still have to do them. My loving husband talks about taking our kids to roller derby or violin lessons as a "grim obligation." It's not that he doesn't love our kids or is unwilling to do the work of parenting, it's that his understanding of love is to do the thing that's needed whether or not he wants to do it. The 8 percent of our student body who are black are viscerally aware that their feelings about police brutality or matriculation rates are brushed off like so much lint. In the political world, our feelings are bandied about by every whim of doctrine, and it seems everyone who wants something preys on our feelings. What use could they be, if our emotions can be toyed with so easily?

But that's precisely it—they're of huge importance, which is why politicians toy with them and why we need to turn our attention to our feelings to take our own inner lives seriously. Our feelings aren't shameful or irrelevant, but it's much easier to cram them the hell back where they came from and pretend they don't exist. We don't even know we're doing it. "Conceal; don't feel," Elsa of Arendelle famously said. That doesn't work for most of us. We still feel them, and trying not to makes it worse.

We have a right to feel whatever feelings bubble up— they're just there, they're not morally good or bad. But feeling them doesn't mean giving them free rein. Having feelings is not a "license to inflict them on others," to quote psychoanalyst Selma Fraiberg.[5] The feelings themselves, as intense as they can be, are just arrows pointing toward something else. As I said before, my anger generally points to sadness, so whenever I feel a hot spike of anger, I try to ask myself what I'm sad about. If I'm angry at politicians, I'm usually sad about the people who are hurt by their policies. If I'm angry with my children, I'm usually sad I haven't been a better parent. Comics artist elodieunderglass says, "Thank you, anxiety. Thanks for making sure I always try my best," and, "Thank you, jealousy for showing me my own needs and ambitions and helping me to name them."[6] Anxiety and jealousy teach her about something deeper. The point is, your feelings just are. They exist within you like your blood and teeth, neutral and useful. Let them do their job instead of weaponizing them.

I've been feeling my feelings a lot lately. At Walt Disney World last summer, I started weeping at the dinner table when an innocuous conversation about our favorite smells—tomato leaves, onions cooking, certain shampoos—turned suddenly to my husband's future death and my future inability to change my bedsheets because they'll smell like him. More mundanely, I've noticed a sense of goodwill and even enchantment toward the people I happen to be around, brought about purely by the fact that they exist. I've felt the hurt of an insult instead of intentionally ignoring it. I've been able to feel my feelings more and to name them better ever since a pilgrimage to Germany in 2017. Some students and I were journeying to places of spiritual significance in Munich, Augsburg, Neuschwanstein, and Taizé, France. The very first day, we went to the Dachau concentration camp memorial. Dachau broke me open.

It's not possible to describe what it's like to be in a place like Dachau. I imagine the new national lynching memorial in Alabama is similar. Dachau is a place heavy with death, heavy with cruelty, and it is a place of ridiculous beauty. The day we were there, the sky was perfectly clear and blue, the trees lining the center road that had been planted in 1933 were a healthy several stories high, and birds were singing in their branches. But we walked through the gate that says *Arbeit macht frei* (Work will set you free), and I knew just how much of a lie that beauty was. I stood in front of the filing system with little cards for each prisoner who had been inside the walls and that had been kept in careful order by some of those same prisoners. I accidentally walked the wrong way through the building with the ovens and came upon the gas chamber unexpectedly; I all but ran through it to escape its claustrophobic walls.

And then I found the back gate that led into the silent chapel of the Carmelite convent that had been built just on the other side of the wall only eighteen years after the camp had been liberated. These women live only steps from a place of such suffering. The nuns' presence, the presence of Nazi and victim, the presence of so many beautiful lives before and after the war, all made this ground holy. I wanted to take off my shoes for the holiness rose from the ground in waves. Of course, this doesn't mean it's all fine—it may never be fine. Holiness means *set apart*, not *okay*, and for me, it means *filled with the lives of beloved people*.

Friends, my heart broke; I wept for most of the time I was inside those walls. And my heart broke open; it wasn't only sadness or disgust I felt, it was awareness of humanity's cruelty, indifference, and resilience. It was awe. Everything I'd seen there, everything I knew about what had happened there rushed through me as though I had no skin. My heart was broken open, and I began to feel everything I'd kept hidden.

The difference between heartbreak and being broken open is when you're broken open, you can't entirely close up again, or as Leonard Cohen wrote, there's a crack where the light gets in. It's painful, but it's also so freeing. Picture the beginning of *The Sound of Music*: Julie Andrews on top of the hill, her arms flung wide, the camera spinning around her and taking in both her delight and the splendor of the mountains from every angle, but you know she's not really happy at the convent, and the Nazis are coming soon. It's like that.

This is why we feel our feelings: we become more compassionate to the whole world, and compassion changes things. I know it may sound naïve in a world such as this, but it's true. The harder we try to control things, to reshape the world in our own image, the less we see what other people need. Compassion for the world removes the barriers between enemies and friends and opens us to possibility. The energy we've spent on hiding or protecting or lashing out we can spend on creating and inviting. We can look back and see just how constricting it was to keep our feelings at bay.

This is how we do it. I call the process "What am I feeling? What do I want?" First, feeling your feelings means seeing them, naming them as they're happening, even if it's only the happy/sad/angry trifecta. This is, honestly, the hardest part, and one I come back to over and over. If this is all you can manage right now, good on you. Next, it means being gentle with yourself and anyone else caught up in the maelstrom of your feelings, not lashing out or insisting on your way. Then, look for what the feelings are pointing to—what do you need? And then it means letting them go, not pretending you don't feel them anymore, but releasing your hold on them. Buddhist tradition asks us to neither cling nor reject nor be indifferent. It's a weird paradox that the more we allow ourselves to feel our feelings, the more freedom we will have from them. (Let me just say, I know that some of you are experiencing certain mental illnesses, and letting your feelings in can actually make you less well. If that's you, know that I see you, and that your feelings will be there for you if and when you're in a healthy place to embrace them.)

We can make this process easier by doing some small spiritual experiments. Ask yourself who in your life you trust with your uncertainty and your fear. Tell them that you trust them and why. Consider activities or experiences when you remember crying or laughing so hard you cried. Don't try to recreate those experiences completely, but do try similar things again and allow yourself to feel whatever comes up without judgment. If you know a difficult conversation is coming, give yourself permission to feel the thing you're actually feeling rather than defending or lashing out. Next time you're angry, examine where in your body you feel the anger—breathe slowly and cradle it there with your mind. If you've already done some work on feeling your feelings, try sitting with the patterns you have for rejecting them or clinging to them. Do you see yourself responding better to them in certain situations? Maybe none of that works for you. The point here is to be intentional, to practice feeling and responding.

The more you practice feeling your feelings and opening up to compassion, the better you get at it. It's the same as practicing anything—the more you practice bowling or playing piano, the easier it is. When you practice feeling and naming your feelings, you'll build community around you who are doing the same. The men in our community at the Edge House have developed a culture of vulnerability where they feel supported to explore their feelings and to talk about things they can't with other men. They push each other to speak their truths and to ask for what they need. They frequently say how much they love each other and why. Some of them are physically affectionate with each other, a desperately needed skill in modern America where homophobia and transphobia are barriers to intimate male friendships.

You don't have to go to such extreme lengths as visiting a concentration camp to help break your heart open. I went to see Radiohead in concert recently and was reminded of the amazing communion that happens at rock shows or in clubs. When I feel the bass reverberating through my body and everyone is singing along, when I hear the harmonies interweave, feel them vibrate in my chest and bounce around my brainpan, I breathe more deeply, and space opens up inside me, like my body contains infinity. That night at the Radiohead concert, Thom Yorke came out with just his guitar, and the five thousand of us in the stadium sang over and over, "For a minute there I lost myself, I lost myself." It was transcendent. Singing at the Edge House on Sunday nights opens me up just as much. One of my favorite songs, sung in three-part harmony, goes like this: "What we need is here; what we need is here." Everything we need is already here. You have what you need already, here in this melody, here in these people, here in your own heart where you've got these mixed up, confusing feelings. What we need is here; what you need is right here.

# 7

# Say the Thing

> Have courage and be kind.
> —Ella's mother, *Cinderella* (2015)

Near my house is a business called CBT, which could stand for anything really: Consolidated Bifurcation Transfers, maybe. Their motto on the sign is Solutions on Demand. I imagine myself going in and banging my fist importantly on the counter, demanding a solution to climate change. Before you get grumpy and say, "Actually, a simple internet search shows you they're an industrial equipment manufacturer," I know that. I googled it myself. But isn't it interesting how many businesses, pharmaceuticals, and even churches have names that don't give you any clue what they are? I find the name of another of Cincinnati's businesses refreshing for this very reason: Aluminum Extruded Shapes. You absolutely know what you're in for there. They extrude shapes made of aluminum. Need a shape extruded? They're your guys. Shapes, extruded to your exacting, shapely, aluminum specifications. The name says what they're about.

There was a whole era in the nineties when churches and youth ministries all had gritty names with weird punctuation like TheGathering and more:room that didn't tell you anything about what they were or what they did. When I started at my campus ministry, it was called The Edge, and the motto on the website was "on the edge of campus, on the edge of faith, because Jesus is the edgiest one we know!" I need to be gentle with the crafters of this motto because they were doing their best to say the thing. We are indeed on the edge of campus, and we are, if not edgy, on the funky end of spiritual communities. If I'd thought of it then, we might have changed the name to something like Welcoming Campus Ministry, because that's who we are. Instead, we ended up adding to it a little—it's now called the Edge House: a campus ministry gathering place. The name tells you exactly what it is.

In the UK, they say, "Does what it says on the tin." At the Edge House, we call this "Saying the thing." It's a technical term, of course, complex and nuanced: it means be who you are and say what you're about. The problem is we don't often know who we are or what we're about. I went to visit with my bishop one day to talk about the Edge House and the future of the church and other weighty matters about which—surprise—I have many opinions. I was in the middle of a story when it suddenly dawned on me: he was really listening to me. I mean, what else would he be doing? And, with horror, I thought, "What am I saying?"

If you're like me, you haven't fully examined what is important to you and why before you open your mouth. "Because I said so" isn't just a perfectly legitimate parenting tool, it's also a defense mechanism we all use to avoid the consequences of what we think. Immigrants are dangerous, because I said so. Because that guy on TV said so. A sprawling federal government is a good thing, because I said so. Because my parents said so. The authority we lean on is our own, which is notorious for not being particularly clear or humble. We want things, we think things, but we don't know why, because we're spiritually asleep.

---

You'll notice as you read that this chapter and the following one, "Ask for What You Need," are very similar, a hairsbreadth apart even. This one is about articulating your own truth, regardless of how beautifully you say it or how fearful it is to do so. The next one is about relying on each other and not being able to live our lives alone. One is focused inward, the other outward, but they're both necessary. They need each other to function, like humanity and forests need each other to breathe, or like I need cookies to live.

---

It starts with how we talk about things. You've heard people speak euphemistically to make something easier to talk about. We call a prison a *correctional facility* and genocide *ethnic cleansing*. We don't say someone's died, we say they passed away or we lost them. The worst euphemism I ever heard was when I was nine-months pregnant with my son: the doctor at my weekly ultrasound called me into her office to tell me I was at risk for "pregnancy loss." That is not even a little bit comforting. It's not that the terms are wrong but that they hide something. They hide the physical and emotional reality; euphemisms hide the bodies.

More than simple word choice, we often use manipulation to get what we want rather than just coming out with it. We cloak our desire in an avalanche of words that talk around the thing instead of just saying it. Asking someone on a date involves a surprising amount of equivocation—even for the most confident among us. Politicians are skilled at not answering the question they've been asked and turning it around to their talking points. There are religious folks who, with the best intentions, try to get college students to join their group or to get baptized in their tradition but use a bait and switch to get them there. Here's some free food, now let's talk about Jesus.

I had a student years ago who was excited to spend his spring break on another college campus winning souls. He told me about the survey that they used to talk to other students. It started with innocuous questions about what the students were studying, what they thought of various amenities on their campus, and then switched to whether they'd made a commit-ment to Christ. This and every one of the above manipulations are well-intentioned attempts at being less confrontational, to protect the speaker from backlash, but they all shroud their meaning in darkness. When we do this, when we hide our meaning, we hide ourselves.

This is all a defense mechanism because even when we do know the truth about ourselves, we're afraid to say it—afraid of judgment, afraid of giving something away, afraid of an argu-ment. You might not think of yourself as fearful, but I invite you right now to put down this book, to sit in silence with yourself, and to ask, "What am I afraid of?" Be honest—you're the only one who will hear. And don't stop at the first thing or at things like needles or heights. Try rephrasing the question to, "What's holding me back from saying or doing this thing?" Whatever that is, it's a defense against being known.

See, saying the thing is not just honesty—though I hear it's the best policy—it's clarity and simplicity. You might feel a swirling miasma of emotions that is the very opposite of clar-ity and simplicity, but being able to say "I'm feeling a lot of things right now that are hard to sort through" is huge because, in doing that, you're not enmeshed in the feelings. You have a little distance from them, even if it's only an inch. I call that the meta conversation, others call it self-observation or awareness. You can talk about the actual content—your swirling miasma of emotions themselves—or you can take a step back and look at the fact that you're having emotions. That's the meta level.

When I first started doing campus ministry at the University of Cincinnati in 2009, I had only a handful of students. Four, actually. And they were great people. I loved talking with them and learning about what they were learning. But there was something missing. I was building this community from the ground up as an experiment. My hypothesis was, if I really pay attention to what the students need and create space for them to get it, we will grow and be fruitful. It struck me that these four students, and probably others, might benefit from regular group conversations around accountability and difficult questions, but how to sell them on it? It doesn't roll trippingly off the tongue, and anyway, I'd need to convince them with clever wordplay. I went to my spiritual director, a wise and calm woman named Julie, and said, "Julie, I want to invite these students to a weekly group where they're expected to show up and not be on their phones. We'll talk about current events and theology, and I'll really press them on what they struggle with. It'll be hard and rewarding. How do I say it so they'll do it?" She said, in her calm, thoughtful manner, "Can you just say that?"

You can do that? Just say the thing in all its awkwardly phrased and unfinished glory? Yes, yes you can. I asked the students in precisely those words, and they immediately agreed.

It's daunting to just come right out and say the thing. "I like you" shouldn't be that difficult, but I struggle with saying it to my new friend Annie, who I like very much. It's hard to say to a coworker, "It makes me sad when you talk to me like that," "I'm confused about why this was offensive," or "I think we should plan the project this way," because it allows for the possibility that you're wrong. You're revealing your soft underbelly to someone who may take a stab at you. Why would you ever bother to be clear and upfront?

You may be reading this and thinking I'm buck wild for saying this is hard. You're a straight shooter; if anyone asks, they'll get your honest opinion no matter what. Maybe so, but I've met a lot of self-proclaimed straight shooters who don't actually say the thing at all. When it comes down to it, they obfuscate like the rest of us. And even truth-telling can be self-protective, a cloak to keep anyone from looking any deeper.

Now, I don't want to be too hard on us—this isn't a black-and-white proposition. A lot of the time, we speak truths and do ask for what we need. It's a process of liberation, and one that gets easier with practice. The street preachers who come to campus think of themselves as straight shooters, I imagine. They're so damn earnest when they yell at us that we're all going to hell for being gay and wearing yoga pants. I think they're honestly trying to save people's souls and come at it from a place of love. I can't imagine any other scenario, really. But they never say that part, they never open themselves up to say, "I'm worried about you, friends, please listen to me," or "I don't like yelling at you either, but I'm supposed to do this or I'll go to hell, too, and I'm afraid." There's no conversation, no depth, no connection.

To be fair, saying the thing doesn't always go well. One of our alumni dated a lovely man who was mystified by her ability to name what she was feeling and to ask clear, incisive questions. He was so used to game-playing and defensiveness in his romantic relationships that her openness was strange to him, strange enough that he ended the relationship. Don't worry, she's fine, dating a stellar guy who appreciates what she's practiced, but this is a good reminder that no matter how open and well-intentioned we are, some folks won't be ready for it, and conflict might arise anyway. Many of us have experienced saying the thing as the prelude to an argument that we'd just as soon avoid, thank you very much. When we get angry—I can speak from experience here—it's yet another defense mechanism against the vulnerability we feel. If you speak to me honestly, it might break open my sense of being right or comfortable, and I don't like that. But a confrontation where we say the thing with an eye to better understanding doesn't have to be a knock-down, drag-out fight; it can just as easily be calm and considerate if we're intentional about it.

There may be times when formal language and carefully thought-out wording is important—negotiating a nuclear peace treaty, say—but it's less often than you think. There's a year-long program on our campus that students apply for called the Racial Awareness Program, though now they also talk about gender, sexuality, class, ability, and all kinds of other things that cut deeply into who we are. Students from various backgrounds and identities meet weekly to learn and discuss and be challenged. It can be a contentious space as the scripts the students have been living with their whole lives come up against something new. One of their guiding principles is to be gentle with each other as they speak imperfectly about what they see. In practice, that means not policing how something is phrased when the speaker is struggling but sincere. Instead of demanding everyone fall in line with a particular understanding, they learn to ask questions and speak their own truth without judgment. They are learning to say the thing. Talking about identity and privilege and politics is anything but clean and simple, and yet it can be done without the cloak of defensiveness.

Last semester, some students and I were on campus with our Red Couch and our chalkboard that said, "Rant to us about religion. We'll listen." A guy walked by, read the sign, and then said with disdain, "Brainwashing," and kept walking. I could have tried to get him to stop to try to convince him he was wrong about us. I could have chased after him to berate him for his rudeness. Instead, I nodded and sighed and said, "Yeah, sometimes it has been." I heard him from several feet away say, "Wow." Now, I don't know if that was a sarcastic "Wow" or if he was surprised by my candor, because he didn't stop. But in that moment, he answered our written question honestly from his experience, and I answered his implied question— "What are you going to do if I call you on your bullshit?"—with my own honesty. Yes, religion has been about indoctrination, Christians have a lot to answer for, and I don't see any reason to try to hide that. We both came at it without a mask. He said the thing and I said the thing, and I like to think we are both the better for it.

What if we take as our model for action the Cincinnati Art Museum's signage? Museums have signs all over the place telling you who sculpted the statue and where the restroom is. It's necessary and helpful and usually boring. The CAM is a beautiful, venerable building, so they didn't want to put up big, obvious signs on poles, nor did they want them to be so subtle and blend in to the walls so as to be useless. So, they designed simple, eye-catching banners that run along the baseboards and are connected by a thin line to a hand-sized asterisk at eye-level, kind of like a footnote. The banners say things like, "Restrooms are about thirty seconds away. You can make it," and, "Asia is all the way down the hall on the left just past all this Greek stuff." I seriously wish every building in my life had footnotes.

What's helpful about them is they're friendly, especially to first-time museum-goers, and they explain simply what you need to know. Yes, you can touch this artwork. No, don't take flash photography. Yes, it is culturally awkward that the British Museum has pieces of the Parthenon that belong to Greece. I don't expect you to paste signs to the knees of your trousers explaining your feelings, but what if we dropped the pretense and said plainly what's going on?

Practicing saying the thing invites us first to consider what's on our mind and heart—what is the thing we need to say? The more we practice saying it, the easier it gets, and the more we invite others to do the same. Have courage, be gentle with yourself, and just say it.

# 8

# Ask for What You Need

> Find your voice and use it.
> —Mark Hunter, *Pump Up
> the Volume* (1990)

What do you need? Right now, I could do with a hummus on rye with those little pickled onions and maybe some sprouts. So maybe I need lunch. I also need to get more sleep. I have a friend who's a sleep specialist who says, hands down, absolutely no one gets enough sleep. Right on, sister. I'm exhausted. So, I need to go to bed earlier, put my phone down sooner, that sort of thing. But more than that, right this moment, I need to look around me and be present to my life as it is rather than how I think it ought to be. I spend a lot of time trying to fix things and to make others see things the way I do, trying to be in control so the entire world will do better. I need to call up my centering prayer refrain, "Be here now."

At the end of almost every conversation with students, I ask them what they need. You'd think they'd be ready for it by now, but it usually catches them off guard. Their first answer is usually, "I don't know." And then it's, "I just want this pain to be done." And then, "I really need to go write that damned paper and get it over with." And then, if we sit long enough, it becomes something like, "I need to forgive myself." Sometimes what we need is obvious and sometimes, not so much.

---

Just like in the previous chapter, "Say the Thing," there are two parts to asking for what you need: the first is figuring out what you need, the second is asking for it. There's an additional part, maybe part 2.5, which is acknowledging that "no" is a legitimate answer.

---

This past year, I asked one of my students, Natalie, to be my administrative assistant for an hour a week. She would make sure we sent out thank-you notes to our dinner-church cooks, send a weekly announcement email to everyone, and remind me periodically to create an alumni newsletter and to set up alumni events. I couched all this by saying, "I'm not going to want to do the things you're asking me to do, but I need someone to remind me." I thought this was what I needed: a pleasant and consistent reminder. About a year later, the things she was reminding me to do weren't done, she was miserable, and I was oblivious. To her credit, Natalie said the thing to me: she said she didn't feel appreciated, she felt futile because I never did what she asked, she didn't want to keep doing this job. I needed to hear that. Basically, I had asked her to be a professional nag. I hadn't asked her for what I really needed: an assistant to actually do the things.

But how do you know what you need? It's so easy to confuse needs and wants, and even to be oblivious, like I was. Asking yourself what you need involves peeling back some of the layers I talked about in the "Take Off the Costume" chapter. You've got your unmistakable needs, like physical safety or thirst. And, to be fair, lots of us are terrible at noticing even those (now is a good time to go drink a glass of water; hydration is cool, friends). Just underneath those immediate physical needs, you have deeper needs, maybe to be right or to experience pleasure or to have more information. These are real needs, but they're also still fairly surface ones; they're the bottom of your emotional hierarchy of needs. Or, to put it another way, those immediate emotional needs cloak the deeper, more complex needs underneath. This is the bit when you strip down to your skivvies. When you start peeling back your emotional layers, you'll discover other needs underneath: a need to be good, a need to trust, a need to be needed. Figuring out what you need requires self-observation and honesty. Let the question of need sit a little, let multiple answers rise to the surface.

Needs and wants, as many financial gurus and evangelists for decluttering have said before me, are not the same. I need to eat; I want that hummus-and-pickled-onions sandwich. I need love; I want it to be from Benedict Cumberbatch. Asking for what you want is a good practice, too—there's nothing wrong with wanting something—but it's hugely important to know the difference. This is one of the reasons we're so big on teaching about consent on college campuses. Sexual assault is horrifically common on campuses nationwide, partly because people don't know what it means for someone to consent to sexual activity. Consent is verbal, sober, ongoing, and enthusiastic. You may want to have sex with someone, but you don't need to have sex with them. And, no matter what brought you to this point, you don't deserve to have sex with them. It's a question of what you do with that feeling of wanting.

It's entirely possible that when someone asks for something they need, we can't give it to them. "No" is an acceptable answer, either because the person doesn't have the capability to help, because they're emotionally exhausted, or because they just don't want to. We all have agency—that is, we can make choices; we have power over our own lives. Just as we have agency to ask, we have agency to say "No." So, like recognizing the difference between our needs and our wants, the question becomes what we do with that "No." In seeking justice, you could pester the person over and over to give you what you need—remember Jesus telling the story of the widow who pestered the unjust judge until he gave in because she was annoying. In seeking a romantic or sexual partner, you should trust their "No." You could ask yourself what you actually need, like I did with student-worker Natalie—perhaps you need something else they can say "Yes" to. Or, you could ask someone else—getting a ride to your doctor's appointment is a clear need, so maybe you just need to find a willing person. Someone's "No" isn't the end of the story, it's more information—what do you do with it?

Recently, there's been a flood of videos on social media of white people calling the police on people of color entirely unnecessarily: she was at her neighborhood pool and he didn't think she belonged there; he was minding his own damn business waiting for a friend in a Starbucks. Watching these videos is instructive. The people calling the police think they need one thing: to assert their superior understanding of what's legal or acceptable. "I'm just making sure; it's important we all follow the rules," they say. What they miss is that most of the people they're worried about *are* following the rules, but they're doing it while black. When I watch these videos, I see white people who are feeling uncomfortable, who have been socialized to find this person's skin color threatening, who want to be right or who are so uncomfortable with the possibility of being wrong that they double-down on their assertions. I also see people who are letting their own wants get in the way of another person's needs, namely their need to be seen as a whole person, not as a problem. What the folks calling the police need is to see past their assumptions, to ask themselves what's making them uncomfortable. They need to examine what they want and find a different way to respond to it.

When I do premarital counseling with a couple about to get married, one of the tools we practice for a good relationship is active listening. Sounds thrilling, doesn't it? One person asks the other for something they wish they'd do more, for example, "I wish you would empty the dehumidifier buckets in the basement more often." The person being asked is the one listening actively, so they respond by rephrasing the question to make sure they understood it: "You would like me to pay more attention to when the dehumidifiers are full and empty them, too, because they fill up fast and we don't want the comics down there to get moist. Is that right?" Arguments happen primarily because we assume the other person knows what we need and is being a jerk and not doing it. Because we don't understand what the other person is asking us for, and just as much because we don't say the thing and ask for our own needs to be met, we jump into the deep well of resentment and violence.

If the first step is discerning what you need, the second step is asking. Obvious, right? But it's not. We spend a lot of time assuming people know what we need or assuming we know what they need. It's incredibly awkward. What if the other person laughs at us? What if they say no? I was incredibly awkward, back in the day, asking people out. When I tried to ask the boy I liked to prom, there was so much hemming and hawing and vague disclaimers that it's a wonder he knew what I was driving at enough to turn me down. Asking someone out is a deeply vulnerable thing, even if you're practiced at it. And sometimes it's a little ambiguous whether it really is a date. One of our students talked about going on what he'd thought was a date only to discover partway through that the woman he was with already had a boyfriend. In that scenario, their need was for clarity: instead of asking, "Wanna go see a movie sometime?" ask "Wanna go see a movie sometime as a date?" or even, "Is this a date? Because I'd like it to be." Say what you mean; ask, so expectations are clear.

I have a good friend who used to manage a schmancy restaurant. They made tasty food, but, like everyone, sometimes they screwed up. She was happy to do what she could to fix things when that happened, but there were many days she'd come home frustrated because someone had sent an angry email or left a caustic post on Yelp about what a terrible experience they'd had. "Why can't they tell us something's wrong when they're here and we can do something about it?" she'd moan. Maybe it's because they get a visceral thrill from complaining and being vindictive, maybe they don't think anything can be done, maybe they're nervous about speaking up in person. The point still stands: if you want something to be different or better, why not ask? Worst case they say no, and then you can still write your scathing review and entertain your friends and family with yet another customer-service disaster story.

I met a university staff member for coffee one day to talk about his life. This is what my job really is: I drink a lot of coffee, I play a lot of board games, I talk to people about their lives.

Anyway, we talked a little about his and his partner's religious backgrounds and he said, like a lot of LGBTQ folks I've talked to, he still believed in God but felt entirely alienated from God's people. Too many sermons condemning him, too many snide comments and assumptions about what he wants.

Even so, he missed church. He and his partner longed for a community of faith where they would be loved for who they were. I suggested several congregations in town known for being gay-friendly, including the Metropolitan Community Church, a denomination founded in 1968 specifically to minister to LGBTQ folks. He said, "I appreciate what they're doing, but I don't want another gay man telling me God loves me. It's weird, but I want a straight person, someone part of the establishment, to tell me who I love is okay." So I told him so. Because I believe it with all my heart and because it's true. I said, "God loves you both. God loves the love you share. You are doing what you're supposed to do, and you are welcome in God's community, whichever one you choose." His eyes filled with tears and then so did mine. I'd had no idea what he needed before he came in that day, but because I listened to him, saw him as he was, he was able to ask for what he needed. And because he asked, I was able to meet his need, which made us both shiny, happy people.

We often think we can guess what another person needs or what they're thinking just by looking. Sometimes that's true—I can tell when my students are upset just by looking at them. They think they hide it so well, but they all show it right there on the surface. What do they need, though? What are they upset about? That, I have no idea without asking. You might be talking to someone and notice that they look super grumpy. You'll assume it's because they disagree with you, or think you're stupid and hateful or the T-shirt you're wearing is just the worst, when they're actually only hungry. Or that's their thinking face. There's a guy in my congregation who, when I preach, sits forward with his forearms stretched out across the pew in front of him and his head bowed forward. When I first started there, I was nervous, so I thought he was angry and trying not to show it. Then I thought my sermon was so boring he'd gone to sleep. I eventually figured out it's actually his listening pose, cutting out distractions. He's listening intently to everything I'm saying.

Let me be clear, I'm not talking about respectability politics, that is, asking politely for what you need and prizing politeness as the highest good. Some needs are so deep and painful that a polite request won't cut it, especially when we're speaking about something bigger, like acknowledgment of our country's racist history or justice after a mass shooting. Asking a government to give you what you need is, at best, a fool's errand given its size and impersonal nature. People of color in this country have been asking nicely for decades to be seen as people and for their experience of discrimination and abuse to be redeemed. There's a point at which the asking becomes more strident. Protests after every unarmed black man is shot are the people asking, demanding, requiring what they need after they've been told no over and over. These are not, as some would say dismissively, tantrums from entitled children. They are the expressed pain of the victims of abuse who won't take it anymore. Asking for what you need is precisely what groups like Black Lives Matter and the Parkland students are doing, what teachers rallying across the country for more funding are doing: collectively asking for safety, for their lives to be taken seriously regardless of race or age, and asking for it in a louder voice.

I suspect white nationalists, men's rights activists, and other exclusionary groups are also asking for what they need, but in response to a painfully distorted understanding of the world. It looks permissive and aggressively weird to them. It looks threatening, as though offering women, LGBTQ folks, and people of color equality and opportunity means there's less to go around. Their thinking comes from a place of scarcity rather than abundance. But it's not pie. It doesn't run out. These groups think they need a return to a safer, simpler past, one that never actually existed. They want to be free to laugh and love and build lives of their choosing just like the rest of us. We're not really that different. Perhaps what they're looking for, what they need underneath all the hateful rhetoric, is assurance that they are also valuable human beings, that they, too, are worthy of love and belonging. Asking for that, and offering that, can change everything.

One of our students, Ophelia, has struggled for some years with serious depression and self-harm. It comes in waves, she says, and sometimes the wave almost drowns her. Recently, she started to open up to another student who really wanted to help but felt out of his depth. He came to me to ask what he should do. Right off the bat, you notice that they both asked for what they needed. Good for them. When Ophelia and I got together to talk, she was well and truly pissed off at the other student for sharing her story with me. She felt betrayed and embarrassed. She was afraid we would abandon her. I wonder if she didn't also feel frightened of the possibility that things could change.

We get so used to our wounds that, even though they hurt like hell, we'd rather cling to them than step out into the unknown. Healing can look threatening. We ignore our needs because we fear change: the actions we take to make things better might not work, and if they do work, how the hell do we function in this new world we've helped create? How do we trust the new health will stick around when it's slipped through our fingers in the past like sand through a hourglass?

When I asked Ophelia to consider seeing a psychologist, she was firm that she didn't want me to bring it up ever again. Only a few days later, she texted me saying she might have been too hasty, and she'd be willing to talk to someone. I felt such relief in that moment and such pride that she was willing to return after everything and ask for what she needed, even though she didn't know what the future would look like. I went with her to the appointment. The counselor she saw was so, so gentle and helped Ophelia see a little of the heart of her sadness: if people really saw her, the real her inside, they'd run away. This is, of course, a lie we all tell ourselves, but for Ophelia, it was all she could see. It was a great cloud that blinded her eyes and stopped her ears from the awareness that there was anything outside it. She couldn't see how beloved she is, how much of a blessing she is to us and her family and the world.

Here's the good news: only a week later, she was humming and smiling as she worked in the Edge House kitchen because her new medication had started to work and because of that, she was starting to see the sun breaking through the clouds. Of course it's not the end of her story—things will go up and down, medication isn't the only answer for her or anyone—but it's good practice reminding herself that she's not in this alone, that she can ask for what she needs.

Another of our students, in the midst of a conversation about body image a few years ago, said, "You're allowed to take up space." She meant that women are often pressured directly and indirectly to be smaller, thinner, to take up less space in the world. But she also meant that all people are literally three-dimensional, that your body is what it is, not what you think it's supposed to be, and that your opinions and needs are not nothing.

Now is a good time (again) to drink a glass of water and contemplate what you need: time each day to rest, courage to say the thing, more green vegetables in your diet, energy to help combat climate change or respond compassionately to the refugee crisis. There's a whole world of possibilities available. What speaks to you?

# 9

# You're Involved, Not in Control

We demand rigidly defined areas
of doubt and uncertainty.
—Douglas Adams, *Hitchhiker's
Guide to the Galaxy* (1979)

"Could you talk to Richard Spencer?" asked my new friend Ryan.

You know who he is, right? Richard, not Ryan. Ryan's a higher-education professional and a stand-up guy; I think you'd really hit it off. Richard Spencer, on the other hand, is one of the new faces of white supremacy in America and recently failed to speak on the college campus I serve. Maybe you've seen a video of him being punched in the face? Or the one of him being maced in Charlottesville? Or spouting absolute nonsense? Honestly, I hope you don't know who he is and he's faded into deserved obscurity by now.

Right, that guy. Anyway, could I talk to him? I think I could, and here's why: I know I can't change his mind. Any conversation we might end up having would not end in a tearful change of heart on either of our sides. I could talk with him because I know I'm not in control, I can't convince him of anything. He thinks what he thinks, and I really enjoy delving into what people think, paying attention to their body language and asking difficult questions. Door-to-door Christians who come to my house get a lot more than they bargained for, which may account for why I haven't seen them for a while. I think I could talk to Spencer because I can take him seriously. Which doesn't mean I approve of a single one of his beliefs, but I could sit across from him and listen for his pain. Perhaps that would be enough.

Oh, but I want to be in control. I want to fix all the things. It's a reassuring illusion that I could do just that. The world is broken—just look at it—and I can see how it goes back together. If you'd just follow my instructions instead of your own desires, we'll be put right in a jiffy. Failing that, I want *someone* to be in control—someone I like and trust obviously, not your guy—but no one is. Not presidents or prime ministers, not bishops or imams, not the police or the military, not your parents. We're making this shit up as we go along, and every time we think we're in control, that we've figured it all out, that's when we're about to slide back into chaos.

It doesn't even have to be the vast, institutional things we want to control. How many times have you vowed to get more sleep or to break some obnoxious habit like biting your nails? It doesn't work in the long-term because we come at it from a place of control: "I'm in charge here, I'll make myself do the thing because it's important—ooh, cookies . . ." We think we're in control and then we beat ourselves up when we fail. While I have a word or two I'd like to share with Saint Paul in the here-after, he nailed it when he wrote to the church in Rome, "I do not do the good I want, but the evil I do not want is what I do" (Romans 7:19). Willpower alone just isn't enough. We are not in control of anything. Control is an illusion.

Powerlessness is strangely helpful, because it means I'm not expected to be in control, I'm not expected to fix everything. I find great comfort in that. One of my most favorite bits of the Jewish Bible is a long poem about powerlessness that most people I meet find exceptionally depressing. Every time I read from it, my anxiety flows out of me effortlessly like the syrup in the middle of a chocolate-covered cherry. It's the book of Ecclesiastes, written by Qoheleth, "the teacher." We don't know who this teacher was historically—the book itself says it's King Solomon, but many scholars aren't so sure. I like to think of her as a thoughtful, curious, insouciant woman. Qoheleth has tried everything at least once in search of joy and satisfaction. She writes that she has spent considerable time and resources on pleasure, but "all is vanity and a chasing after wind" (Ecclesiastes 1:14). She has pursued laughter and wine, which also are vanity and a chasing after the wind. She tries great works, gardens, possessions, wealth, entertainment, even despair and folly, and all of them, everything she chases, turns out to be wind: uncatchable, incorporeal, futile.

She writes, "It is an unhappy business that God has given to human beings to be busy with" (1:13). And, "They all have the same breath, and humans have no advantage over the animals; for all is vanity. All go to one place; all are from the dust, and all turn to dust again" (3:19–20). Is it any wonder my friends all think this book is depressing? But let's be honest with ourselves, there are times we need this reminder that we are made of earth, that the things we're so damn proud of creating will not last, that we are not, in fact, gods—all-powerful to remake the world in our images. We don't claim to be all-powerful out loud, of course—we're not monologuing supervillains—but we think it, even if it's just in reference to our own backyards. It's so freeing to know that we don't have to build the best tower or write the most amazing book or make the greatest country— that's not our job. Our job, according to Qoheleth, is to eat and drink and find enjoyment in our work. That's it.

Now, I know most of us aren't thinking about building a huge tower with our name on the side or whatever, but we attach ourselves to control just the same. I was in a class on mindfulness, and a woman was sharing some of her story and weeping a little. The woman next to her looked around a bit frantically for some tissues and wrapped her arm around the weeping woman. Our teacher asked her why she did it. She said, "Well, she was crying. She needed to be comforted." Our teacher said, not unkindly, "You don't know what she needed. What you did comforted you." I see this all the time—in myself, too. We feel uncomfortable in the presence of someone's pain, and we want to do something, take away their pain, make ourselves feel less uncomfortable. But it's all awkward, and we can't control it.

Several years ago, I took some students on a pilgrimage to Denver and the Rocky Mountains. We had planned to visit and worship with a church we'd admired for years and to do some volunteer work for the nearby Boulder Parks Department. Later in the week, we would drive into the ridiculously gorgeous mountains and hike on trails four-feet deep with snow and covered over with a thick layer of ice. I really dislike planning trips and making reservations, but I persevered, and we had our itinerary. It was all under control. Until it wasn't. First, I got sick on the plane because I figured I didn't need to take my anti-nausea drugs, having not been motion sick in years. Which was because I always took my anti-nausea drugs. I lay on the Denver airport's stylish and surprisingly comfortable carpet trying to keep the world from spinning for half an hour before we could leave. Then there was a hiccup with the car rental, the story of which is only interesting after a couple of cocktails, but since I was still ill while we figured it out, only added to the sense of chaos.

Once we were ensconced in the church basement where we'd be sleeping for the week, things evened out. But then on our second day of work, there was a sudden blizzard in Boulder, and we were told not to come in. Now what? It's not the worst thing that could happen, but we didn't know the area and what to do with our time. I'd heard the local children's hospital had a neat chapel with a labyrinth in the floor, so we decided to go walk it. A labyrinth is kind of like a maze, but it has only one path. It's not about finding your way but about walking the path set in front of you—again, no control, no decision-making, just one foot in front of the other. This one was small, intimate, and our time walking it was marked by silence and calm.

Over lunch, we decided to go find a second labyrinth we'd heard was in the area. We arrived at the address we'd been given to discover that the labyrinth was inlaid in the vast marble entryway of a huge office tower. To walk it meant to pause every so often when people who worked there walked across the floor. Off to the left was an expansive, amazing art gallery. While we were there, a young man, an elderly woman, and a medical aide came in and gathered around a piano in the gallery. The young man played classics from the American songbook while the woman beamed at him. Turns out, all the art in the gallery had once belonged to the old woman, and her husband was the building's developer. Her husband had designed the building as a tribute to her. Ever since she'd developed Alzheimer's, her husband had paid a pianist once a week to play for her here, among her paintings. Not being in control began to look more like a surprising gift.

We piled into the car to return to the church on whose basement floor we were sleeping only to discover that once a week, the church, too, had a labyrinth available for people to walk, laid out in cloth on the floor. So we walked it. We couldn't have planned a moment of this day, and it turned out to be one of our favorite days of the trip because we were not in control. Things happened and, because we were not attached to a plan, we went with it.

I could take credit for this transformative trip, talk up my stellar decision-making skills, how well we have created a culture of listening at the Edge House, how self-aware my students are to choose the labyrinth over, say, a movie. And there's truth to all that, but I wasn't the only one in charge. Other people were there, too. Sometimes I feel like the only options are to cling to my success or to reject it. Cling and reject, cling and reject—it's enough to make you seasick. But I didn't make it happen nor was I useless. I did my bit, I didn't do all the bits, and that's usually what's needed.

This is what the first-century rabbi Tarfon was getting at: "Do not be daunted by the enormity of the world's grief. Do justly, now. Love mercy, now. Walk humbly, now. You are not obligated to complete the work, but neither are you free to abandon it." We are not in control of the world, of other people, of ourselves. We are not in control, but we are involved.

Perhaps you are thinking this seems pointless—if nothing is under our control, why do anything? But our goal is not to be productive, it's to participate. There isn't a single, universally agreed-upon end goal for all of humanity with a to-do list we can tick the boxes for. There's only the world as it is and the possibility of being part of where it goes. In my stewardship sermon each year (*stewardship* is a church word for *fundraising*, and I do indeed preach basically the same sermon every time) I say, "There is no obligation here. There is only the invitation. You get to participate in what we're doing." And in recovery programs, we talk about doing the next right thing. Not the next twenty right things that take you flawlessly to your end goal, but the next one, the one in front of you right now. To me, this is great news—not depressing, but freeing.

When my students struggle with what they'll do with their lives or with their deep-seated sadness, I want to fix it. When I'm in conversations about food insecurity or sexual assault on campus, I want to fix it so much. When herds of students stop to watch and heckle the street preachers who come onto our campus to tell us we're going to hell, I want to fix the preachers, but I also want to fix the students, so they ignore the hate. I sure as hell want to fix gun violence in America. When students discover more about themselves and are full of joy at what they've discovered but also turn that discovery into a weapon against everyone else, I want to fix it. But it's not about fixing because none of those realities are actually broken. They just are.

I'm not going to lie, I struggle with this idea that things aren't broken. They damn well look broken. Of course suffering should be attended to, but we spend a lot of time with the word *should* in our brains judging us for all the ways we've failed to control the world: I should have a better job, I should be better at meditating, we should have figured out climate change by now. What if we thought in *coulds* and *cans*: I could have a better job, I could be better at meditating, we can work on climate change solutions now. Jesuit priest Anthony de Mello wrote about the things in our lives that give us pain, that look irreparably broken: "If you understood them, they'd change."[7] What he meant was, the more you work on understanding the things you struggle with, the less control they have over your life, your perspective on them changes.

Before you tell me that this is a flight of fancy, I'm not saying your individual understanding changes the entire system, but it can change your little corner of it. Chris Magnus was police chief in Richmond, California, for nine years, and in that time he took the town from the country's eleventh most dangerous city to entirely off the top twenty-five. During his tenure, the department didn't lose a single officer or kill a citizen.[8] They did this because Magnus understood policing and violence differently. Under his leadership, they practiced community policing, de-escalation, and critical thinking around officer-involved violence to learn what not to do. Richmond isn't perfect, and racism still exists in this country, but Chris Magnus's willingness to involve himself in a messy conversation means this one town has changed. It's not that things don't need fixing but that we need to stop trying to get to the solution right away. Being involved instead of in control means we might not see things through to the end, but we can do our part.

That *what if* is important; it's the crux of the idea of possibility and involvement as opposed to control. What if we look at the problem differently? What if there is more space than we expected here? There was this bus stop up the street from the Edge House that was abandoned and in disrepair. I called the city bus folks, who said it didn't belong to them. I called the university, who said it didn't belong to them. I called the City themselves, who said it didn't belong to them. So I called it a public art gallery, and a student and I began collaborating on a project we called the Chapel of the Abandoned Bus Stop. She drew five simple images of scenes from Jesus's life, and we traced them onto tall, thin pieces of muslin. Then we started painting them like stained-glass. It was enough of an undertaking that other students asked if they could help. Soon, we were working on it during our dinner-church, all during the week, and eventually everyone who went on our spring-break trip that year pitched in. If the two of us had tried to maintain control of the project, it would never have gotten done, and it would never have been as beautiful as it was.

We cling so tightly to the way things have always been done, even if "always" is only our own memory, and our clinging only crushes what hope there is. It makes us sick to maintain such control. Anthony de Mello says the cure for our sickness is to look, because "you lose control of the life that you are so precariously holding together." Looking, seeing with open and compassionate eyes, not immediately reaching for a solution, this is healing. It means we lose the false life, the life where we pretend all the time and beat people up over *shoulds*. Even Saint John of the Cross, imprisoned by the men of his own religious order back in the sixteenth century, curled up in his fetid, miserable prison box, wrote some of the most transcendent poetry to the possibilities of the Divine. Misguided and preposterous? Maybe, but also inexplicably freeing. Looking for possibilities is not without risk.

I've fantasized about ways to shut down the street preachers who come on our campus and shame them into never bringing their gross theology onto our campus ever again. This is my desire for control. Instead, I take my own megaphone onto campus and tell the students who pass how much I appreciate their hard work, how I hope they remember everything they need to today, and how much they are loved. I tell them I'm sorry for all the ways the church has hurt them and for all the ways the church has strayed from the path of love over the centuries. I confess our corporate sins, from the early heretics to the assimilation of native peoples into whiteness, all in the name of the church. I call it positive street preaching, and it's a way of joining a conversation already in progress. This is my attempt at being involved, at not clinging but inviting.

We all have our work to do, work we are not obligated to complete but that we can't abandon. What is yours?

# 10

# If We Eat Together, We Will Not Betray One Another

> Your great mistake is to act the
> drama as if you were alone.
> —David Whyte

My husband and I used to go to this amazing Eritrean restaurant called the Blue Nile. The food is thick, spiced stews of lentils or fish or lamb served on a huge and colorful common plate on top of an equally huge, thin bread called *injera*. It's part crepe, part sourdough, and part sponge. Everybody at the table eats with their hands, scooping up the stews with pieces of *injera*. In Eritrea, it's customary for people to scoop up the best bits of a dish and hand-feed them to their loved ones. One of my favorite dishes is called *doro wat*: chicken leg with the meat absolutely falling off the bone in a spicy red sauce with whole, hard-cooked eggs. It's forking amazing. I was always a sucker for the salty, buttery lentils. It's like a less-soupy Indian curry or a gloppier version of baked beans, only completely different.

The man who owns the Blue Nile is possibly the most hospitable person I've ever met. The very first time we showed up, having never laid eyes on us before, he came forward with his arms wide open and said, "My friends, welcome, it is so good to see you!" He thanked us for coming to his restaurant and solicitously sat us on low chairs around a tall woven basket that would later support the communal plate. We thanked him and then he thanked us. He brought us water and mango juice moments after we'd sat and helped us understand the menu. We polished off the enormous plate of food very quickly, and he was so pleased and proud of us for the good work we had done. You know, proud of our work eating delicious food. He thanked us again for eating, we thanked him for making it, he thanked us for our kindness, we thanked him for having the restaurant in the first place, and it continued on like this. We were all so pleased about everything. Each time we went, we watched him do the same thing with every group that entered the restaurant.

What has stuck with me through the years, besides his overwhelming delight to share with strangers, is something from the front of their menu: a description of the giant plates and the baskets they sit in and why they eat communally. It said, "If we eat together, we will not betray one another."

We all know what it feels like to be betrayed. When someone you trust—someone you care for and are vulnerable with— rejects you, tells your secret, or doesn't stand up for you when you need support, you feel shocked and hurt. When families who are meant to love each other unconditionally don't just argue—arguments aren't the end of things—but compromise each other's safety, kick kids out of the house, or turn a blind eye to abuse, you feel empty. When friends say things that cut deep into our insecurities, we feel wounded. If it's not immigrants we distrust, it's the media or our politicians. We distrust our neighbors' motives when they offer us something. When someone dislikes us for whatever reason, we begin to mirror it back, even when we have no other reason to. We take things— parking spaces, self-determination, children—and are shocked when folks are upset with us for it. Betrayal can come in many forms and is painful every time.

Eating together is not magic; it doesn't fix everything in one fell swoop. Would that it were so. The relationships that are nurtured when we eat together can go either way. But notice, betrayal requires a depth of connection that we don't have with strangers. Some dude on the street might be rude, but he's not betraying me. Judas Iscariot, the man who betrayed Jesus to the authorities, was one of the inner circle, had been chosen by Jesus himself, and had spent the last three years of his life living with Jesus and the other disciples. His actions were a betrayal because of how close they all were, how much they trusted each other. If they hadn't cared for each other as they did, it would still have been hard, but it wouldn't have cut so deeply. The inverse of the Eritrean proverb would seem to be true: if I'm going to betray you, I have to eat with you first.

In Eritrea, sharing and loyalty go hand-in-hand. You could read that a couple ways. One, that we are loyal to those who are generous with us, and it encourages our own generosity. Or, two, that we are generous with those who are loyal to us, keeping them close with favors. There's a pretty significant difference between the two, and they often overlap. We humans have a hard time discerning our own motives, and they're just as often mixed as they are pure. "If we eat together, we will not betray each other" is both a description and a demand.

It reminds me of the story in Genesis (chapter 24 if you're reading along at home) when Abraham asks his servant to swear an oath by putting his hand under Abraham's thigh— only, it's the Bible, not known for its clarity of diction, so it doesn't mean *thigh*, it means *genitals*. Probably, they were both cupping each other's genitals as they swore the oath, standing very close, looking each other in the eye. They were swearing on something important—their penises were their manhood and the origin of life, after all. It was even more sacred than swearing on the Bible in court is now. They were also saying, "If you break this oath, I have power over your body, your pain, and your progeny." It's mutually assured destruction. If we eat this same food, we won't poison each other.

I suppose this is a good first step, but I want more than "you won't poison me." Eating together provides an excuse for curiosity. I don't mean accusing questions about how the hell you could think whatever nonsense you do. I once asked a friend why he supported politicians who were clearly doing evil; it was not helpful. And I don't mean invasive, demanding questions as though we're entitled to the answers. People's ancestry or genitals are not yours to examine. Neither of those kinds of questions is curious, they're self-interested. Curiosity is focused on the other person: imagine Mr. Rogers's actual interest in how the other person thinks or Bob Ross's sense of wonder at making mistakes. I mean asking someone what their favorite food is and then asking follow-up questions about how it makes them feel and who they share it with because you are interested, not because you want to argue. I mean talking about difficult things like politics and religion in a way that allows for disagreement. We joke at the Edge House that my pastoral go-to is, "Interesting. Tell me more." I say some variation on that all the time. Kindness and compassion and even changing the world have to be based around curiosity or we have nothing. And it's all made easier when you have food in front of you because you don't have to worry about what to do with your hands.

True curiosity and listening can encourage trust, which in turn encourages love and commitment. It's a process that we will succeed and fail at; it's not magic. This phrase, "If we eat together, we will not betray each other," is already true in many parts of our lives, but in so many others, it's not yet true, and we want it to be. It's something we hope for; it's aspirational. In the Hebrew prophetic literature, when it says "you are called" or "you are saved," the phrase is not singular, like "you, Alice Connor," it's plural. It's a call to the whole community. A better word—and I really am mystified about why translators don't use it more—is *y'all*. Not you, y'all. Not me. We. It's a hope, a promise, a mission. So many times, we've failed each other, and when we look back and see it clearly, we say, "Never again." Perhaps the next step is to say, "Let's eat together, so that we can learn not to betray one another."

In the midst of the United States' immigration dispute, an artist known as JR invited people on both sides of the border to lunch. In October of 2017, JR built an enormous picnic table crossing the border fence between the United States and Mexico in a town called Tecate. It was meant first as a symbol of unity and of community despite nationality, but it quickly became a literal feast among nations—"The Giant Picnic," JR called it. Hundreds of people on both sides of the border brought their lunches and ate at the massive picnic table. An impromptu band assembled on both sides of the fence and played. The artist himself shared a cup of tea with a border-patrol agent. JR expected the table to be removed quickly, as such things are typically suppressed because they're embarrassing to people in power, but it stayed up for hours.[9] The folks who participated didn't just eat together—though that was beautiful in itself—they came because they were curious, and the experience expanded their understanding of who *we* are.

In the end, what we are talking about with love, trust, curiosity, and feeding each other is hospitality. It's a hospitality that goes beyond a "Welcome to Applebee's" or a mint on the pillow. Hospitality is about making space for each other. When we're talking to folks in a hallway, making sure our circle of people always has a hole in it so someone can join in; when we know someone is not on the traditional gender binary, using their pronouns appropriately; when someone tells you something of their life, listening, asking them to tell you more. You can sit in silence and observe with gentleness and still be a part of the community, holding the group in your heart with love. Hospitality isn't just in a hotel or your home. You can be welcoming and curious at work or while waiting for the bus or in your classroom. And in all those places, whether there's actual food or not, we share ourselves, our souls and bodies.

Because humans are a people in process and not stuck in a binary of solely trust or distrust, we eat with each other or are in community with each other or work together with mixed feelings. Sometimes we've already decided not to betray, and we cannot imagine bringing injury. So we eat together to cement the vow that we won't. Sometimes we eat together as part of learning how to trust. It's a vulnerable thing to cook for someone or to be cooked for. What if they don't like it? What if they don't like me? This is not about a corporate dinner or an enforced meal with distasteful family, though transformation can happen anywhere. This is about choosing to eat together, cooking for each other, choosing to spend time over something we have to do to make it enjoyable. It's about inviting the other person's whole self to the table.

Over the summer I was writing this book, a beloved member of my church community died. Judy was an older woman, but still young to have died. She was hilarious and full of energy, ready to take on the entire unjust world. Everyone who spoke at her funeral talked about how she filled their lives with joy. She used to come up to me at church, eyes sparkling with mischief, voice serious, and say, "Alice, what are we going to do about this messed-up world?" I sat in the balcony at her funeral, where I had a full view of the congregation. The place was packed to the gills. I saw all kinds of people I loved, people who were always helpful and championing the work of the Edge House, and people with whom I had some tension. A couple of summers ago, I preached a sermon that a few folks felt was too political and even insulting. They were very unhappy with me. I saw them there at Judy's funeral and had a sudden, beautiful moment of wholeness as I looked at that sea of heads below me—every one of these people is beloved by God and by me. We don't always like each other, we often don't agree, but we are the beloved community, loving each other even when we drive each other up the wall, loving each other because we have experienced transformation when we do, loving each other because we eat together each week.

Most churches celebrate the Eucharist in some form or another—the bread and wine or crackers and grape juice, whatever that community dictates. Our celebration of the Eucharist is based on the Last Supper—the dinner Jesus and his friends ate the night before he was crucified. Which was, I assume, a real dinner. Hummus and tabbouleh, tomatoes and cucumbers and garlic, and syrupy baklava after. It's still called a meal now even though you get more of an hors d'oeuvre than dinner, but it's strangely filling nonetheless. It's not just about the food but about all the freight that food carries. We are eating together and remembering all the times we've eaten together before. We remember as though we were there with the man Jesus and experienced everything he said and did. We taste, just the tiniest bit, what the world could be like.

At the Edge House, when I was figuring out how to be a community before we had any people to make one, I knew we needed a weekly gathering with food and prayer. Typically, that's a traditional worship service followed by dinner. But the Edge House is an actual house, and doing a traditional service in the living room or kitchen seemed a little odd. So, remembering that the Last Supper was an actual supper, I crammed the major elements of a worship service into the form of a dinner. It's church during dinner. Dinner-church. Around this table, the centerpiece of our lives together, we listen to what people are saying. We disagree, but always with respect and usually with more questions. Tell me more, help me understand. People who might not normally talk to each other, people who are suffering, people who are celebrating, people who don't believe all this God nonsense and people who do, people who see the world could be kinder. It's countercultural in a world where we are constantly trying to convince other people of what we think is right.

Our regular meals change how we act at other times. At our monthly board-game night, I usually order Sicilian pizza from this amazing local joint. Their red sauce is thick and tangy and so, so spicy. I always include a veggie pizza in the order, but one Friday, I thought, "There's usually a lot of veg pizza left over, so I'm going to order Hawaiian instead." (Pineapple belongs on a pizza. Fight me.) Of course, that was the night that our new vegetarian friends from India came to play games. I felt terrible. While I was trying to figure out what to do, student Elizah got to work in the kitchen. We had fresh tomatoes and basil from the garden, pasta in the pantry, and some parmesan and other veg in the fridge. She made them a delightful, vegetable-filled pasta that they loved. This is not unusual for Elizah—she's studying at culinary school and cooks for everyone who comes in the door if they so much as look at her sidewise. She makes pancakes and bacon at all times of the day and challah and other fancy breads to practice her skills.

Not everyone in the house can cook like that, but the rest of us make a point to offer craft espresso or tea or even a glass of water to anyone who comes in the door. We recently planted a bunch of blackberry, blueberry, and hazelnut bushes along the side of the house as a free orchard. These things are all our form of Eucharist: we give thanks for this fruitful world, for each other, for strangers, and we share a meal, even if it's only coffee. Each time we do so, we take a step closer into the beloved community and toward never betraying each other again.

I don't think there's a real distinction between Christians and non-Christians when it comes to recognizing our common humanity. Love, trust, and curiosity are universals, but that doesn't mean they're easy. Humans have struggled for centuries to be compassionate. If we allow the stories of separation and inhumanity to define us and our enemies, we will never make it so. Eating together helps us tell a different story, one that mirrors back to us our humanity. Who do you need to eat with?

# 11

# Consider the Lilies, Dammit

> One of the astronauts said, when we originally went to the moon, our total focus was on the moon, we weren't thinking of looking back at the Earth. But now that we've done it, that may well have been the most important reason we went.
> —David Loy

My students make a lot of fun of me when we go on retreat to the woods because when we hike, I stop suddenly every several yards and bend down awkwardly to get super close to the moss. I gently touch it with my fingers and mutter, "Wow," and "What a good little moss you are." Come to think of it, it is a little weird. But moss is amazing, did you know that? They don't have seeds, they have spores that they eject into the wind using compressed air at thirty-six thousand times the force of gravity. There are over twelve thousand species of moss, and the ancestors of current mosses played a large part in creating the ice age of 470 million years ago. Lots of folks know about peat moss used in making Scotch whisky, but did you know native peoples in the northern Americas used dried moss as a kind of diaper for babies and for absorbing menstrual blood? They so did. Oh, hey, I'm doing that thing my students make fun of me for.

On these retreats when I wax rhapsodic about moss, the main purpose isn't about the moss itself but what it represents. Moss is tiny and inviting. To really see it, you have to get down close to it, really look to see the kinds of leaves and texture it has. Retreat is meant for us to slow down, to really look at our lives, to get out in the natural world and let it lead us. My students and I spend so much time deeply focused on computer screens and the expectations of the syllabus or of church council that it seems as though that's all there is to the world. Our upstairs brains tell us, of course, that's not the case. The world is huge and full of possibility, and so much of what they're learning in their classes and at the Edge House shows us how huge and amazing the world is. Yet our daily practice, what we actually do every day, is to narrow it all down to the one thing we're worrying about right now. And the next thing. And the next thing. And back to the first thing. It's exhausting.

The university's art and design school, DAAP, is just across the intersection from the Edge House, and we go over there regularly to give away free craft espresso from the cart we built. Over the years, we've seen an unintentional culture develop: the students don't leave the building for days because of their workload. They routinely stay up for more than forty-eight hours at a time preparing projects or go for a week with only a couple hours of sleep each night. They order in food. They sleep on improvised hammocks if they sleep at all. It's kind of a badge of honor to have stayed in the studio the longest. I once found my student Hollis at the Edge House with pieces of a model for the furniture design project she'd been working on all semester. She was holding out two small, laser-cut pieces of wood and staring at them intently but also with an air of deep melancholy. When I checked half an hour later, she was in exactly the same position. I asked what was wrong, and she said they were due the next day, she'd made a mistake in the machining specs so they didn't fit together, and she hadn't slept for two days. I often think of her despondent face when everything around me is pressing in and I can't imagine it getting better.

There's a joke about nighttime over at DAAP: the building is mostly windowless and constantly lit with fluorescents, so when you're inside, you can't tell what time of day it is, except around 11:00 p.m. when the janitorial staff slightly dims the lights. They call this *DAAP night*. When the lights come back up in the morning, it's *DAAP day*. These students, bless them, are so focused on the work they love, but they're also so focused on the artificial—fluorescent lights, model-making chemicals, creating art to meet the approval of their next critique—that they don't see the wider world, sometimes for days at a time. Their programs are so stressful and sometimes arbitrary that all they want to do is finish. They've learned a lot of things there, but they haven't learned how to deal with stress or anxiety in any way other than pushing through it. It's like they're carriage horses on a gentrified downtown street—the blinders next to the horses' eyes keep them from being distracted by cars and people, which is helpful for the horse, but not all the time, and also we're not damn horses. There's so much more to be seen.

I feel anxious about a lot of things. Will people still like me if I speak up about injustice? Will my kids grow up to be generous and kind but also steely in the face of oppression? Will I have enough money for a comfortable retirement? Should I be giving more money away since Leighton and I really do have plenty in the grand scheme of things? What is this lump in my scalp? Will Americans ever truly look at ourselves and our history clearly and stop being so shitty to people of color? Will the world become a post-apocalyptic wasteland because of climate change, and have I equipped my children to deal with such a scenario? Did I set my alarm to the right time?

I don't know what your anxieties are, dear reader, but I know you have them. We carry them around like luggage with broken handles and a bum wheel wherever we go. We can't let them go because what if we need them? But carrying them all the time is exhausting. We all get caught up thinking it's our work alone in the world. We need to worry about these things to keep them from happening. Because that works.

So, when I take students on retreats, we don't have a plan or structure or expectations. We go hiking and cook together and sing and sit around talking. When we hike, I remind them at the trailhead that we're not trying to get to a destination— the falls or the peak or whatever will be there whenever we get there. Try strolling for a bit and noticing the plants and rocks around you. Try breathing from the bottom of your belly and really smelling the forest. Try noticing how your feet hit the ground when you walk. We stop the frenetic pace of our regular life to really look at the world around us, to smell the smells. We invite each other to stop and smell the roses. (Good right? I just came up with that right here.)

There's this bit in the Christian stories about Jesus where he says something very similar. He says, "Consider the lilies, how they neither spin nor weave, but I tell you, Solomon in all his glory was not arrayed as one of these" (Luke 12:27). This comes right after he's said that worrying doesn't make the future safer or longer, so don't bother. I have always understood these together as Jesus himself judging me and saying I should just stop worrying and be happy. It plays right into my need to work harder and longer. And into my shame that I can't do it. Jesus says, "See those worry-free flowers? Be like them," and he wags his finger at me. Okay, sure, I'll just stop being anxious now. No problem. Do I sound grumpy? I am a little. Because the truth is, just pausing and smelling a damn flower won't fix everything.

And yet, that's not what Jesus is saying. Artist Makoto Fujimura thinks Jesus is offering us an antidote to our worry: the opposite of worry is looking at flowers.[10] It's a deeply unproductive activity; it activates the beauty and pleasure and rest centers of the brain instead of the hurry and accomplishment centers. Jesus says, "Feeling stressed? Go chill in nature. Even if that nature is the one tree near your apartment. Go sit near it. Feel the bark. Look up into the leaves. Breathe slower." Rather than being a comparison or a judgment, it's profound advice.

Many of the things we worry about are legitimate—bridges do, in fact, collapse, and we ought to take more preventative care of them; group projects often fall apart because someone doesn't carry their own weight; there are actual white supremacists advocating for racial violence—and sometimes worry can drive us to work on the things we can affect. When you're done reading this chapter, go make some lists and take some action. But, mostly, worry is pointless. The vast majority of our worries are just our brains and hearts working themselves into a tizzy over something that just exists. People will like you or not, our kids will grow up with some of the things we want them to have and others we don't, I could just check my alarm.

When you're stressed or anxious or insecure, you feel stuck inside a box: four walls, ceiling, floor, corrugated cardboard, just enough space to turn around, smells a little musty, no possibility of anything outside. Those walls are the expectations we set for ourselves, the abuse we receive from others, homophobia, racism, poverty. To be fair, we get stuck inside a box when we're comfortable as well—in academic circles, we call that privilege. The walls of the privilege box are probably fancier: respectability, responsibility, the inherent goodness of authority figures, but they're just as constricting. It's not that your comfort or happiness aren't real, but they are not all that is. And it's not that your anxieties and the abuse you've experienced aren't real either, but they are not all that is. When the box becomes all there is, we end up miserable.

Jesus telling us to consider the lilies or me (entirely originally) telling us to smell the roses isn't yet another task to check off our lists but is itself the antidote to anxiety—and I love that idea. Literally going and looking at nature makes things better. Not everything and not all better, but it gives us room to breathe and consider the possibilities. It opens the top of the box and shows us the sky that we'd forgotten. There's tons of science to back this up as well. Spending time in the natural world improves our short-term memory, reduces physical inflammation, and improves our sight and concentration. There's even a study in Holland that suggests that the more green space around you, the fewer diseases you'll have.[11]

There are periods in human history when the idea that this would help seems foolish. Persecutions of Christians in the early church, later persecutions *by* Christians, the Armenian genocide, forced labor and chemical castration of gay men—how could connection with the natural world, or anything really, make those experiences better? I think the problem is that we expect something good plus something bad to even out, but it's not a zero-sum game. The horrific exists side-by-side with beauty. There's a cookbook of recipes compiled from women in a Czech concentration camp in World War II. These women, facing torture and certain death, used whatever bits of paper they could find to record their families' favorite recipes. And not only that, they wrote down fanciful recipes, foods they had never eaten and would never eat.[12] They knew there was something outside of what they were experiencing, and they couldn't reach it. And at the same time, they gave themselves room to breathe with these exquisitely painful recipes. Their recipe book written on slips of paper was their way of considering the lilies: there was joy in their midst, the possibility of a tiny, budding flower. Even there, on the threshold of death, is beauty, walking alongside tragedy.

At its base, this may be what Jesus was talking about: appreciating beauty. Or, as my husband puts it, "apprehending aesthetic splendor." We see something beautiful, we want to possess it or take it apart. What about appreciating it for what it is, where it is? DAAP is all about taking art apart and then possessing what makes it beautiful or worthwhile, and for good reason. An art degree is meant to encourage more complex, more beautiful, and also more marketable art, so of course they'd spend a lot of energy on what makes art good or desirable or functional. But there's a step after that: gazing at it with love for what it is.

To consider the lilies is to allow yourself to experience beauty and love. To choose not to experience those things, or to keep other people from experiencing them, that's what theologians call sin. It is a kind of violence we perpetrate because it cuts us off from everything that is. It cuts us off from what fills us up and from what heals us. To choose to consider the lilies is to bring your whole self—all your anxiety, all your work, all your privilege, all your misery—and to look at them all with gentleness and curiosity. To consider the lilies is to choose love. All of it, taken together, suggests something bigger. In my language, the language of the church, that's God. You might also call it your higher power, the universe, that which brings us a sense of love, connection, belonging, and challenge.

It's important to remember that this flower gazing doesn't happen in a vacuum—you're not going to arrive at a perfectly peaceful moment when none of your worries impinge on your consciousness and the Divine is fully present in front of you. It's going to happen in the middle of your anxiety. My Pilates teacher, while we were holding a five-minute plank pose and sweating and swearing and shaking, said, "Notice your muscles, which ones you're using. Keep breathing slowly and be curious." Be curious. Not judgmental, not assuming anything, not constantly miserable, but curious. It's not just about those horrible Pilates poses, being human is about asking questions, wondering, asking what if. Curiosity offers an open sky and lilies swaying in the breeze to a heart that's stuck and stale. For just a moment, we can forget there even is a box.

You can't always control what moment is going to wake you up and let you see the lilies out of the corner of your eye. Sometimes it sneaks up on you. But you can choose to be curious. My student Hollis—the one with the furniture project that wasn't working—came to us as a vocal atheist, clear that we wouldn't convert her. And we didn't try—that's not our job. Over the years, she wondered to herself if maybe she didn't have to be in DAAP all the time, if perhaps she could leave and do other things. She developed friendships outside the building and rediscovered her spirituality. When she graduated, she was rejuvenated; even her posture was more open and calming.

This involves a choice: choosing to leave your classroom or work building over lunch, choosing not to get out our phones or computers every second we don't have something to occupy us, choosing to read something different than our usual, choosing to connect with a friend or family member or talking to someone new, choosing to ask a question to genuinely hear what the answer is. To consider the lilies, and to have those lilies change you, requires you to take action.

The lilies you can consider could be any number of things: You could sit under a tree and look up through the leaves or at the shadow pattern they make on the ground. You could lie on the ground and look at individual blades of grass or smell the leaves on tomato plants. You could look from your car window out and up at the strange overlapping greys and tans on a concrete wall that has been repeatedly graffitied and painted over or whatever else you notice. Because that's the point—noticing.

Pulling back from what you think is the whole world to see even more world. Taking a break from what must be done to see what already has been done.

What is it that fills you up, that makes your breath come slower and deeper, that makes you feel like you could contain multitudes? That is your lily. Go consider it, dammit.

# 12

# Ambiguity Is Neither Good nor Bad

> Just hold on loosely,
> but don't let go.
> If you cling too tightly,
> you're gonna lose control.
> —38 Special

We have a spirited and ongoing debate at the Edge House about what makes something a sandwich. The basic definition is filling between two pieces of bread, but it's never that simple. Does pita count as two pieces of bread? Does a hotdog bun? Isn't an open-faced sandwich still a sandwich? A quesadilla is basically a Mexican grilled-cheese sandwich, and tortilla is basically bread from a different culture, right? Some of the students feel more comfortable with a strict binary: sandwich or not sandwich. I reject that system as too simple—it doesn't account for shades of meaning. I subscribe to more of a Venn diagram of sandwiches, concentric circles radiating out from a central, straightforward PB&J, where things like quesadillas or rolled sandwiches are sandwich-adjacent. Since it has a bread surrounding filling in such a way that it keeps your hands mostly clean, I'm very comfortable calling a burrito a kind of sandwich. Others look at me with horror and disgust when I say that.

I enjoy this conversation every time it comes up because it reminds me how unclear most of our lives are and how much we desire direct answers. It's not just sandwiches. Humans don't like ambiguity. We evolved to need clearly defined boxes, like edible or poisonous, safe or dangerous. Even categories like sacred or profane are necessary social classifications, directing our culture toward the good, or so we hope. Blockbuster movies work their magic showing the good guys and the bad guys plainly so you know who to root for. Lawyers tease out specific, direct answers to complicated questions with the help of laws that are, at best, blunt instruments. Christianity has struggled since its inception with the desire for a clear taxonomy of who's in and who's out—even though God's response to our question of "Who is in?" is either "Everyone's in" or "Wrong question." We imbue the answers to these questions with a moral dimension: things are good or bad and require praise or punishment. But the world is much more complex and undefinable than all this.

Think about the coffee table in your house that you constantly bark your shins on. It hurts like hell when you run into it by accident. You're bringing over a cup of tea or a sandwich to sit with your lovely friend on your equally lovely couch when suddenly that damn coffee table, maliciously lurking where it always sits, takes a bite out of your lovely shins. What an evil coffee table to have hurt you so! On the other hand, its hard surface is so very convenient to rest your tea and/or sandwich on, its sharp corners only doing their best to maintain Euclidean geometry. That coffee table is elegant and convenient, and its hardness is only a side effect of its usefulness. It's a good coffee table. The table itself is just there, minding its own business. It is neither good nor bad, it simply is. It's your attitude toward it that changes depending on what you need. Your experience of it is ambiguous.

Let's take a more complex example: grief. Grief that someone you loved has died, grief that a friend hasn't called back in weeks and weeks, grief that people online can't seem to recognize each other's common humanity. Whatever it is you're grieving, it hurts. The pain you feel running like roots through your body, pulling your energy, your lifeblood, into itself, that pain is neither good nor bad, it simply is. I know, I know, you hate me right now for saying your pain is good. That's okay. That also is neither good nor bad, it simply is. Infuriating, isn't it?

The pain we feel as we grieve a loss is good because it signifies that there was something real in the relationship. It's good because it signifies there was love and care and sustenance. The pain we feel is bad because, damn, it hurts. We are alone, at a loss, confused, empty. And the pain we feel is neither good nor bad. It's actually not possible to make a moral judgment on the pain itself—it just exists. At some point, for whatever reason, it won't exist, replaced by a different pain or by a different joy. We don't like to think of that, particularly if the loss we grieve is a person. As much as it hurts, we want to feel the pain always because it reminds us of who we were when they were here: loved and worthy. But the pain dissipates like wind blowing through a window. Chasing after it, trying to hold it, calling it righteous or evil is neither truthful nor helpful. It just is.

The problem is that pain exists, suffering exists, and we want to know why. The word we use in theological circles is *theodicy*, which asks how a benevolent God can exist when there is so much suffering in the world. The predominant answer now and for the last few thousand years is that it is deserved. If you broke your leg, you must have been doing something you shouldn't have. If you're poor, it must be your fault. And conversely, if things are going well for you, you must be virtuous and a hard worker. This perspective has been around for centuries and across cultures, and it still exists in the Christian church as the core of prosperity gospel theology, which is not only a crock of shit, it's actively hurtful to the people who subscribe to it. The hardest-working people I know are near or below the poverty line, and their pain, by and large, has nothing to do with their morality. Shit happens, the sages say. Rain falls on the just and the unjust alike.

But not everyone agrees with this philosophy of merit—in fact, over the centuries, many have criticized it. The book of Job in the Hebrew Bible lays out a poetic deconstruction of guilt and merit as hogwash: Job's problems are not his fault. Job is a paragon of religious virtue six hundred years before the birth of Jesus with a beautiful house, smokin' hot wife, 2.5 kids, and a Mercedes in the driveway. The predominant thinking, then, is that Job deserves these things because of his virtue. But the story gets complicated. On a bet from the Tempter, God tests Job's faith by killing his kids and livestock and servants, afflicting him with running sores, burning down the house, and salting the earth. Job's "friends" brainstorm what he did to deserve his fate and come up with nothing, because their understanding of things happening for a reason is gravely flawed. They assume he must have done something wrong to deserve his fate, but the story tells us he is blameless. This book, gross and weird as it is, is hopeful, because it is one of the first literary explorations of moral ambiguity. Most people, even then, see clearly that the universe isn't a divine vending machine doling out candy only to the people who have exact, morally upright change. But enough of us want it to be that we make art and books and sacrificial rituals that all tell us in no uncertain terms that it's true.

Job's troubles are not about his deserving them, and neither are ours. The evidence suggests that things are more complex than whether someone deserves something. Sleeping around can lead to venereal disease, but so can trusting your spouse. Investing money in a start-up can lead to financial success, but so can selling drugs. People who do justice, love kindness, and walk humbly with their God get sick and become homeless and have all manner of bad things happen to them. People who do evil get raises and drive nice cars and live delightful lives. And, more than that, we're not one thing or another. We're both good and evil, saint and sinner, sandwich and not-sandwich. The answer to the question of suffering is much more ambiguous than what sin caused it.

One of my favorite words is *liminal*. It means the space between things, literally the threshold of a house, the doorway into something. When you're in a liminal space, you're really in more than one space at once, you are in both rooms and neither room. Things are uncertain, or at least in process. Another of my favorite words, as you've probably surmised, is *ambiguous*. It means uncertain, unclear, equivocal. It has an air of mystery about it, as though each letter is made out of question marks. When things are ambiguous, we humans feel uncomfortable, we reach for a resolution, we step through the doorway instead of standing on the threshold contemplating. But the doorway—that ambiguous, liminal space—isn't a bad thing; it's just a space between things. And it is a space where possibilities bloom.

Imagine a pendulum swinging back and forth, back and forth. When it swings far to one side, let's call that absolute clarity. And when it swings far to the other, let's call that pitch-dark blindness. In the middle, the path the pendulum traverses, is ambiguity. It's a mix of clarity and blindness, of ability and exhaustion. This is the liminal space we find ourselves in most days, with enough clarity to function but just enough blindness to make it difficult. Our churches, our schools, our governments, all our institutions are in this liminal space as well.

When my students and I talk about their lives and the decisions they're making—changing majors, breaking up with someone, what they have to offer a broken world—they are often looking for a single right answer. Since I'm a reasonably functional adult, they ask me what they should do, and I have to break it to them that there isn't a single right answer. There are several right answers; there are possibilities. Their college years are a liminal space between being children and being adults, a space between things, a space to breathe and create, even in the midst of their hectic schedules. They feel dread and eagerness simultaneously. The ambiguity of that, the uncertainty of it, can feel threatening. But ambiguity is neither good nor bad, it simply is. Possibilities are neither good nor bad, they simply are.

We want clarity, and we want it on our own terms. We hold tightly to what we know or what we think we know and make decisions from that clenched posture. It's like we take one look at the vastness of the universe and, instead of feeling grateful or in awe, we freak out about the scarcity of oxygen or water and hoard it all for ourselves. As I wrote in a previous chapter, we are not free to abandon the work of our lives; we are involved, but we are not in control. Binaries and clear categories are one way we try to control the world around us and fail. Have you ever noticed that whenever a religious group talks about the end times, sometimes with a very specific date, and they say only a select few will be saved, it's never some other group who will be selected? It's always that same group, it's always "us." I'd love to see a doomsday cult that operates with open hands, that is entirely certain that only 144,000 will be saved but it's some other group, those folks over there who they've never met and who are frankly a bit weird, but not us.

No, we hold on with clenched fists to what we know about tax law or vaccines or immigration policy or addiction because it gives us clarity, even if that clarity means we're looking at the world through spectacles that need a good cleaning. What we see isn't wrong, per se, but it's distorted; it's not what's actually out there. A mentor of mine once told me perfection isn't being without error, perfection is seeing the world as it is rather than as we want it to be. This is what I mean when I say ambiguity simply is: the world we live in isn't so black and white as we might suppose. It's full of mystery and motion and possibility and that's okay.

Instead of clinging hard to everything, what if we hold it all loosely? Think about a pretty leaf that your child or friend has given you for safe-keeping on a long walk. If you want to keep that leaf for them, you have to hang on to it, but you can't crush it. You have to hold it loosely, maybe in a small cage of fingers, maybe just on the edge. If you hold it too loosely, it might blow away, but it would still be intact. If you hold too tightly, it's ruined. Now imagine someone you love in the place of that leaf. You want to hold on to them, to keep them near because you love them. But you can't crush them with your arms; they would leave for fear of suffocation. Hold them loosely.

Embracing ambiguity instead of trying to stuff everything into labeled boxes is all about opening up possibilities. It's invitational: because there are multiple right answers, choose one, follow it with gusto, and hold it loosely so that you can choose another answer when you need to. If you hold on to your imagined result too tightly, you make all other good results impossible, and you probably won't get the result you want anyway. Some call this the grey area, some people call it nondual thinking, and some call it hopelessly relativist and thus the devil's work. Ambiguity is not about not making a decision, it's only recognizing that things are messy.

If things are messy, then what we rely on are kindness and experimentation. Kindness because we all need it, even that one guy you can't stand. Especially him. Experimentation because it's a way to sort through the possibilities while not clinging to any one of them.

To lean into ambiguity, you could try calling God *she* and notice what happens inside you when you do. Then try calling God *they*. You could read up on policing and race and try to put yourself in the shoes of someone who thinks differently than you do. You could call to mind a decision you made recently that seemed obvious and ask yourself what other right answers you could have chosen. You could identify what liminal space you're in right now. My father recently went blind, but it was a slow process—he was partially blind for months and had to learn what his limitations and new possibilities would be. Your liminal space may not be quite as obvious, but I bet you're in one. If not, talk to a college student about the rootlessness they feel and how they bear the temporariness of their life. In any of these, it's important to notice what discomfort you uncover and what possibility you see.

Another way to experiment is to embrace saying, "I don't know." It's a spiritual practice in a world where we seem to be expected to have an opinion on everything that happens, whether or not we know anything about it. Scientists make their livings investigating things they don't know. Art collectors and anthropologists, economists and meteorologists, all look at their bit of the world and say, "I don't really know. Let's look more." On the BBC show *Doctor Who*, the Doctor is thrilled when she runs into something she doesn't understand. Why wouldn't we say the same thing in our spiritual lives? It's not that we know nothing, but there is so much that is a mystery, so much we are drawn to and don't fully understand that we can turn over and over in our brains. Saying "I don't know" with a sense of wonder is one of the best and most potential-filled things we can do.

I don't know what to do about sexual assault on my campus. I don't know how to educate people about consent better. I don't know which group ought to be first responders to the survivors. I don't know how to articulate that drunken sex isn't always assault, sometimes it's just a bad, mutual decision.

I don't know how we stop perpetuating the myth that violence can be redemptive. I don't know how we stop committing violence against each other full stop. I don't know how we learn to see people who aren't us as us.

I don't know how photosynthesis works, not really, but isn't it amazing? I don't know what makes little kids get excited about storytelling or making art or cuddling, but off they go! I don't know why Caravaggio's paintings make me breathe more deeply.

Neither does anyone else, not for sure. Because there isn't only one right answer. In all of these we are standing in a doorway with a multitude of possibilities flowing through us. Each of these scenarios points to something more; each moment of pain we experience points to multiple solutions. It's not clear which way we ought to go, but when we step through the doorway, we make the path just by walking it.

# 13

# Everything's Awkward. Lean into It

> How you think you are: a hot, messy, truck-fire of a person who disappoints people.
> How other people think you are: cool and fine.
> —Kristin Chirico, "13 Charts That Will Make Total Sense to People with Imposter Syndrome," BuzzFeed

Some people think I'm very cool. They see the tattoos and my work with millennials and my ludicrously high energy, and they think, "That's a cool lady right there." They couldn't be more wrong. I'm a giant dork. I play *Settlers of Catan*. A lot. I tried to start an *X-Files* fan club in college to which no one came. In high school I was really into tea etiquette and knew the old English system of currency by heart. I missed being valedictorian by a hundredth of a point, and I'm only grudgingly okay with it now. My husband and I have a habit of mugging for the camera like the cheesy ending of every sitcom in the nineties— there's no camera, it's just us in our kitchen. Even my tattoos are nerdy.

More than all this, I'm awkward. Gangly even. A few years ago, I had this habit of drawing attention to my awkwardness in an effort to make it less awkward. Take a guess at how well that worked. I would make a double thumbs-up and waggle them up and down, being goofy to dispel any fear. This gesture became a form of loving mockery at the Edge House. I'd announce some upcoming event—Red Couch or espresso carting or giant-sized *Settlers of Catan*—and then instinctively look for their approval with my waggling double-thumbs. They'd do it back and laugh. I asked one of my students from that era, Imogen, what she thought of it. She said, "I think you were externalizing your feelings. You do that a lot, and that sign makes things more awkward, not less." Imogen, who is partially deaf, told me the sign for *awkward* in American Sign Language (ASL) is similar: thumb and first two fingers of both hands extended flat and hands making a kind of bicycling motion. Because the sign for the letter *A* is similar to a thumbs-up, she gave me my deaf-name: the sign for *awkward* with the fingers formed for letter *A*.

All we want in awkward situations is to make it less awkward, whatever "it" is. But we can't. Meeting new friends as an adult, conducting international diplomacy, asking your lover for something in bed, putting together Ikea furniture—it's all awkward.

Dan Savage hosts an advice podcast called *Savage Love* about sex and relationships all across the spectrums of sexuality. It's earthy and explicit and, I shit you not, it's one of the most compassionate and thoughtful shows on the air. He's essentially a pastor to his listeners. It's funny, it's heavy, it's brilliant. Most commonly, when people call in to ask how they can do one thing or another, the thrust of their question is how to do it without it being awkward. "How can I break up with her without it being awkward?" You can't. "Is the first time I get tied up for sexytimes going to be awkward?" Yes. "I want to tell my partner how great they are but it's awkward." Sure is. The content of their questions almost doesn't matter because awkwardness cannot be avoided nor successfully boxed up. Anything that's worth doing is uncomfortable at some point.

In Christian churches, it's traditional to wash each other's feet on Maundy Thursday, the week before Easter. There's a whole story about it in the Bible where Jesus tells us to do it, just like he tells us to bless and eat bread and wine each week. There's no soap or a nice sugar scrub involved in this foot washing—there's just water and a towel—but it's more symbolic of our serving each other and being served than about actual cleanliness. At my last church, people resisted my suggestion that we add it back in to the Maundy Thursday service. They said, "It's weird. People don't like having their feet touched." That's the point, I said. It's supposed to be uncomfortable, at least the first few times you do it. It's intimate, awkward. Even Saint Peter didn't know what to do with it when Jesus came to him at the Last Supper. First, he refused to let Jesus do it, then he demanded Jesus wash not just his feet but his head and hands, too. Panicked babbling, if you ask me. My own experience having my feet washed is one of receptivity in the midst of discomfort. Someone besides my family can love me and touch me with such safety and beauty, and it's possible for me to do the same.

Awkwardness isn't reserved for negative experiences. A good friend of mine, Xander, wrote to me, "The most awkward I've felt, or at least I am willing to admit to, was walking down the aisle single file to marry [my husband]. I do not know why admitting my love to someone in public could be so embarrassing and yet so open. I felt totally exposed." I presided at this wedding, and I can tell you that every wedding has this moment of awkwardness: both people are so delighted to be there and so nervous. It's a thing of beauty.

Whatever you do that's new or unpracticed or intimate will be awkward. That awkwardness stems from an instinct to resist and pull back in fear. I made my hand gesture to ease awkwardness because I was resisting what I assumed were people's judgments. Foot washing is awkward because we resist the exposure and intimacy of that kind of touch. Learning a new skill like a turn-around toe-stop in roller derby is awkward because we are resisting the way we've always done it before. As well as the very real possibility of falling on our asses. The resistance can go both ways: awkwardness doesn't define the moment as good or bad, it just is. Resisting something good like trust makes us more contentious and cut off; resisting something bad like violence can make us freer. Both are very difficult, very awkward in practice because we resist change, we resist being wrong.

My resistance shows up in my body. I'm a very tense person, and I hold tension in obvious places like my neck and shoulders, but also weird places like my hip joints, my forearms, and my butt. So I go to a massage therapist every three weeks to try to let go of that resistance. It isn't awkward any longer because I've been seeing the same therapist for several years now. There have been moments on that table when I thought about how intimate the experience is—decidedly nonsexual, but still very intimate. We breathe together. He feels where the knots are before I even know they're there. He digs his elbow into something heavily muscled like my glutes, and I'm not going to lie, it hurts like hell. But it's less pain and more resistance. What happens is, as he presses in on whichever part of the muscle is tense, it starts shivering. The surrounding muscles lock up to protect it as he zeroes in on the tight part. It feels ticklish and awkward and then suddenly everything lets go. When I'm paying attention, I release my breath and a kind of spiritual tension as well.

It's the same kind of experience when we choose to lean in to something awkward in our lives. Whatever hurts or is scary we protect. Something inside our brains resists the release that's coming and circles the wagons to protect the bit that hurts. We might feel shaky or anxious. Extending the metaphor, if we keep leaning our mental elbow into the awkward thing—meaning we show up for a difficult conversation or we ask the person out or we admit we've made a mistake—the tension releases. It may not be perfect—it's not magic, after all—but the awkwardness begins to dissipate because we've dealt with it, walked through it, rather than running away or pretending it's all fine. It's uncomfortable but necessary for change.

Discomfort is how we learn. A new physical skill makes our muscles hurt and our brain struggle to comprehend until it becomes second nature. Being confronted with our privilege is uncomfortable, but we won't know any better until we wade through the discomfort. In seminary, I worked on revising some preexisting prayers to include feminine language for God as well as gender-neutral language. One of my classmates thought it wasn't a worthwhile endeavor because the prayers sounded clunky and weird. Of course they did, we had been using *he* for so long, it was second nature; anything else would automatically sound weird for a while. But it doesn't last. Practice makes it easier. What starts as uncomfortable and awkward becomes normal with repetition and community support. If something is important to you, it's worth the awkwardness as we get used to it.

There are people in this world who look so damn suave it seems preposterous that they could feel awkward. Celebrities on the red carpet, scholars who excel in one field or another, our next-door neighbors who seem to work effortlessly at their jobs in social justice, whose child is the literal cutest, and who have plenty of time to bicycle in the park for an artisanal picnic—when we look at them with envy, we've completely missed the awkwardness they feel every moment. All those people who look like they've got their shit together, don't. Confidence doesn't mean you don't feel awkward. When actor Andy Serkis was in the motion-capture studio filming The Lord of the Rings, he wore a full-body Lycra suit covered in little black-and-white markers and often had white dots all over his face. He squirmed around the set or in front of a green screen for months, creating the strange, inhuman physicality of Gollum and looking supremely awkward. You can't tell me he didn't feel it, too, but he, like all good actors, was willing to make himself look foolish for the sake of something bigger. You can be confident and awkward at the same time—this, too, isn't a zero-sum game, just like horror and beauty existing simultaneously isn't. Awkwardness exists when we're not entirely comfortable with what we're doing, and confidence comes from trusting yourself, which in turn comes from practice. What we do regularly, what we practice doing, shapes us partly due to muscle memory and partly because we've started to trust ourselves.

Consider the people you look up to and why you look up to them. The things they do well, they've practiced over and over so it looks easy. I still feel very awkward when a student wants to talk one-on-one about what they're struggling with. Are they angry with me about something? What if I can't help? But I've practiced listening and asking questions that draw them into something deeper. With enough practice, it becomes muscle memory. My tiny, scary, German piano teacher used to say, "Amateurs practice until they get it right; professionals practice until they can't get it wrong." Which she said because I didn't practice at all. She didn't mean we can achieve flawlessness; it's meant to make the point that practice makes it easier. Even when we reach a point of mastery over the piano or of naming our emotions or what have you, there are always new questions, new challenges, new, dare I say it, awkwardness.

If we run away from something because we're afraid it will be awkward or uncomfortable, nothing changes. We have to practice being awkward. Or, rather, we have to let the thing be awkward while we practice.

One of our awkward practices at the Edge House is taking our Red Couch onto campus. It's weirdly magical—people talk to us constantly. We've talked about our favorite cheese, about choosing the wrong career, about eschatology and salvation and what street preachers think they're doing. Sometimes people think it's super weird; mostly people dig it. This kind of thing takes practice—to talk to a stranger on their turf, to let yourself look foolish so that people will talk to you. We have had to allow the awkwardness a seat at the table so that we can have these transformative conversations. I typically acknowledge the awkwardness—not with my thumbs-up sign anymore, thank goodness, but sometimes verbally, sometimes just to myself—and keep going. What this does, with practice, is allow other people to feel awkward as well and show people you really see them.

When one of our trans students asked if we would consider inviting people to share their preferred pronouns when we did introductions, I was all for it, but it was very awkward at first. For some folks, the idea of trans identity itself was brand new, so even talking about having preferred pronouns was strange and uncomfortable to them. For others, the fear of misgendering someone was huge, and there were a lot of mea culpas happening. Slowly, we've gotten better about asking and correcting ourselves when we use the wrong pronouns. And it's not because the demon of political correctness has taken over our little snowflake brains. It's because we care about the people in our community, and we've spent time listening to their stories. We've learned how hurtful some words and actions are, and we've decided to try not to inflict more harm. It's about really seeing people and caring for them as part of the human family.

Now, I've already made a distinction between being uncomfortable and being unsafe in the first chapter, but it bears repeating. Feeling uncomfortable doesn't mean you're unsafe. One can tip easily into the other, but they are unequivocally not the same thing. Discomfort means irritating, painful, or uneasy. The level of pain you can withstand and it still be uncomfortable is different for different people, of course, but you'll notice that none of these things are dire. Unsafe means unprotected or dangerous. Hearing about the pain someone with cancer experiences may make you feel uncomfortable; having cancer and not knowing if or when it might return makes you unsafe. To be unsafe is to be immediately at risk for harm or to be beyond your ability to cope. We can still learn from unsafe situations, but not usually until we've put some significant distance between ourselves and them. When it's a government or culture that is making people unsafe, it's important for those of us who only feel uncomfortable not to let it rest there. Leaning into the awkwardness of learning about those who feel unsafe, of calling out bad behavior, of standing up against power can be overwhelming.

Doing something new or learning to do it well usually means discomfort at some point, but the opposite is not true: the presence of discomfort doesn't automatically mean you're doing something well. It's a bit like we say to our daughter, "Art makes a mess, but mess doesn't automatically mean you're making art. Sometimes it's just mess." Street preachers seem to take angry hecklers as proof that they're doing right. Robbing a convenience store for the first time probably includes a certain amount of anxiety, but that doesn't mean it's a good thing. You don't have to chase after discomfort; it'll come whether you want it or not.

Consider what in your life is awkward, what patterns of awkwardness you see. It's probably not as awkward as you think it is, but look at those things gently and just name for yourself that it's awkward. Always ask yourself: What are you resisting when you feel awkward? What are you afraid of? Visualize the awkwardness as a thing: an ugly vase or a nebulous pink shape.

Don't reject it, but don't clutch it to your chest like it's precious either. Just let it sit next to you while you try the new thing. It's all fine.

We have to practice things before they become second nature, and learning to trust ourselves and others takes time. Remember, it's neither good nor bad, it just is. Hold it gently, and if it's not okay, it's not the end. Be naked, rest, fail, feel, listen, lean in toward the thing that feels awkward. It's worth it, I promise. As my student Imogen who gave me my ASL name said to me, "Don't agonize about your awkwardness. It makes you, you."

# Conclusion: So What?

> All of creation is going about
> the business of living.
> —*Courage to Change*,
> Al-Anon Family Groups

One of the most common phrases we put on the chalkboard near the Red Couch when we take it out is "Rant to us about religion. We'll listen." Last year, when a young man approached us with intent in his eyes, I imagined a variation of the jovial and deeply engaging atheist we usually get. He leaned over to his bag, brought out a well-thumbed Bible, and opened to the book of Daniel so fast I didn't see it happen. I thought, "Ah, this kind of rant. Okay." He dove into a long explication of the book of Daniel, with particular loving care given to the numbers and references to time. It turns out, because of some iffy math and a common misconception about what the biblical prophets were doing (hint, it's not telling the future), he believed very strongly that the book of Daniel forecasted some form of the end of the world in late 2017. He was polite, but with the edge of aggression that I've seen before when people try to convince me I'm wrong.

After listening to him patiently, I said, "Let's say all this is true. So what?" I continued, "What I mean is, this belief is obviously very meaningful to you, so what difference does it make to your relationships or how you live your life?" Rather than trying to convince him he was wrong and making the conversation a competition that could be won, I took a step back and asked a larger question. I took him seriously as a person, and I invited him to take off his costume. It's hard to do that in the moment, to engage someone's passion rather than the content; practice makes it easier. We had a nice conversation after that, but he didn't have an answer to my questions, other than to say he'd never considered it. He walked away looking a little disgruntled but thoughtful.

I share this story with you not to mock him and his beliefs—that's too easy and too cruel—but to ask you that same question. "So what?" You can phrase it however you like: "What difference does this make?" "What do you need?" Even, "So, what do we want to do about this?" However you phrase it and whatever it's about, it's one of the most important questions we can ask ourselves in any situation. It's the question that can remind us we have a choice in how to respond.

For example, my dog, delightful as she is, pees on our dining-room floor on the regular. It makes me so angry, but if I can ask myself, "So what?" I'm less likely to yell at her, and I'm more likely to release my anger sooner, because I'm giving myself a moment to choose. Ask yourself "so what" when you're stuck in your feelings because you and a friend are arguing: How exactly is it she hurt your feelings? What does she think she's saying? How do you want to proceed after the argument? When people protest in the streets, ask yourself, "What is it we can learn from them, what is the pain they're expressing?" This is the reflection part of the action-reflection-action model we talked about in the introduction. It's the "why" and "what next" and "what will you do with this." In a world where we have a thousand things vying for our attention, where our every thought can be broadcast immediately, pausing and considering what is needed is revolutionary.

In this book, we've talked about intentionality, new life, participation, community, ambiguity, and awkwardness. We've talked about discomfort and practice. We've talked about experimentation and possibility and freedom. What I want to leave you with is this: how you are is not inevitable. You are not, in fact, strapped in to a cart at the top of a roller-coaster awaiting the inescapable track laid out for you. How you interact with the world can be altered, the scripts you've grown up with or assume are the only ones can be revised. Change is possible. Damn difficult, but possible.

The life you live is not predictable or certain. The life we all lead as humans on this planet isn't either. We can change the way things are by paying attention and asking why and how and to what extent. No one has the right answer, even if they look like they do because they've got money or power or position. We can try out various answers, various ways of being. No matter where you come from or what roadblocks you have in front of you, you always have agency. You can address the ways you ignore yourself, the ways you hurt other people. The "so what" question is much bigger than the words used to ask it. It's about how you respond to the sum of your experiences.

Sufi mystic Hazrat Inyat Kahn wrote, "God breaks the heart again and again and again until it stays open." Our hearts need to be broken open because we keep closing them up tight and wrapping them in layers of bubble wrap and duct tape. Keep out the bad feelings, keep out the potential for pain, keep out knowing and being known. Profound delight can break through those layers, but heartbreak does it so much more efficiently. When my heart is broken by the news or by the pain of someone I love or by my own shortsightedness, it hurts like hell, but the new space created in my heart by that break also lets in pleasure and gratitude. Heartbreak and struggle feel like bad news, but choosing to feel them, to walk through them, means a more open heart, a kinder brain, even for a moment. And that is what will change the world.

Reflection won't take away our pain or solve the immense problems we face. It's not immediately effective or rewarding, but that's not the point. Reflection is about seeing more clearly; it's about opening up and becoming more resilient in the face of pain. Pain and joy sit side by side, neither erasing the other. I'm inviting you to be aware of these two friends sitting at your elbow, to wonder what they have to teach you without clinging to them.

As hard as all of this is, it doesn't have to be miserable. It's weird how we frame the process of becoming a more caring human as an enormous, wretched, inconvenient task, when it's one of the most joyful, satisfying, and necessary things we can do. This can be fun, people! I sometimes take out my frustrations about work and the state of the world on my family. I yell about shoes all over the floor or respond grumpily when asked to help with homework. I'm not proud of it. When I take a moment to look at myself and my family, I realize it's because I trust them with my feelings and exhaustion and imperfection. I trust them not to leave. I still get grumpy, don't get me wrong, I'm far from perfect, but now it's less dramatic, more open to play- fulness. I get a look from the husband that says, "You're doing that thing you do." And I think, "Huh, I sure am." It's like the release of a long-held-in breath or a fiendishly difficult puzzle that you enjoy solving little bits of. It's like the words attributed to master sculptor Michelangelo: "In every block of marble I see a statue as plain as though it stood before me, shaped and per- fect in attitude and action. I have only to hew away the rough walls that imprison the lovely apparition to reveal it to the other eyes as mine see it." And it's like student Nathan's first trip to

New York City and the look of amazement and slight terror as he looked up, up, up at the buildings. Because how we are is not inevitable, we don't *have to* try something new, we *get to*. It's an invitation, an encouragement to take a step out of what we know or what we think must be.

I don't need you to agree with me on everything I've said here, I only want you to consider that there are other possibilities than what you've come to expect, other ways of being than what we've always done. So what? So, this: the world is sometimes shit, being a better human means practicing kindness and awareness, and it's going to be hard. So let's get to it.

# THANK YOUS

My parents always insisted that my brother and I write thank-you notes after birthdays and Christmas. It was the worst burden ever imposed on a human. In the intervening years, I've learned a thing or two about gratitude and am now overflowing with it.

My editor Lisa Kloskin decided, for good or ill, to work with me again. Hopefully she doesn't regret it. I certainly don't. Thanks, Lisa.

Mark Dawes, Kirsten Linnabary, and Annie Esposito read the book and told me it mostly didn't suck. Thanks, Mark, Kirsten, and Annie.

Russell Ihrig works at the Cincinnati Art Museum and tracked down the official specifications and verbiage of their footnote signage. Because I'm a nerd, the files bring me great joy each time I look at them. Thanks, Russell.

Good Shepherd Lutheran Church allowed me a sabbatical in 2018 during which I wrote the bulk of this book. The Edge House campus ministry did without me for the summer, and the house didn't burn down while I was gone, so I call it a win.

The team of people from the church and the Edge House who helped me plan and organize my sabbatical were generous to a fault with their time and care for me. Emily Speck, Amy Schlag, Mark Dawes, Karen Mazzei, Rose Ford, and Andrew Kutcher deserve all the good things you can heap on them. Thanks, everyone.

Friends Jana Reiss, Ross Frischmuth, Troy Bronsink, and Julie Murray and my brother Trevor Van Brunt calmed my tortured soul when I was certain I couldn't write. Thanks, y'all.

Parents Tom and Nancye Van Brunt raised me to argue and apologize and stand firm and say "I don't know." Thanks, parents.

All of my students ever have given me something precious. Wherever you are, whatever you're doing, I love you. And thanks.

Oh, and my husband, mustn't forget him. He's the real writer in our family. He's more than I deserve and makes my life at least 7 percent better. Thanks, Leighton.

# APPENDIX:
# FURTHER PROOF

For your edification, and simply because these are things I consulted or enjoyed while writing, an annotated list of more stuff to help you be a better human.

## Films

*Inside Out*, by Pixar, to learn how to feel your feelings.
*Lars and the Real Girl*, to see how a community responds well to someone they don't understand.
*Pump up the Volume*, to relive 1990 and to get excited about speaking your mind.
*Wit* (also a play by Margaret Edson), to watch self-awareness and suffering and to weep.

## Books

Brown, Brené, any of her books, to be grateful for vulnerability.

Coates, Ta-Nehisi, *Between the World and Me*, to expand what you know to be true.

de Mello, Anthony, *Awareness*, to delve deeper into noticing yourself.

DuPrau, Jeanne, *The City of Ember*, to become aware of the box you're in.

Heschel, Abraham Joshua, *The Sabbath*, to learn about and practice rest.

Lappé, Frances Moore, and Anna Lappé, *Hope's Edge*, to consider how we feed each other and how to see patterns.

Miles, Sara, *Take This Bread*, to consider other ways we feed each other and to read about transformation.

Riso, Don Richard, *Enneagram Transformations*, to begin a journey into who you are and what you need.

Rollins, Peter, *How (Not) to Speak of God*, to speak of God and not to speak of God simultaneously.

Russell, Mary Doria, *The Sparrow*, to have your mind blown and your heart broken open.

Schaeffer, Frank, *Why I Am an Atheist Who Believes in God*, to see the value in atheists and to consider another way to define sin.

Sprunger, Edmund, *Helping Parents Practice*, to be more patient with your kids but also with yourself and the world as we all learn new things.

# Articles

Adams, Christy, Claire Donnelly, Kelly Johnson, Brooke Payne, Austin Slagle, and Sara Stewart, "The Importance of Outdoor Play and Its Impact on Brain Development in Children," UMKC School of Education, https://tinyurl.com/ydy4afjt, to change how we educate kids.

The Edge House, "Rule of Our Common Life," https://tinyurl.com/yamr74un, to read more about the Edge House and what we hold dear.

Morris, Jasmyn Belcher, prod., "Forgiving Her Son's Killer: 'Not an Easy Thing,'" NPR, https://tinyurl.com/y8wzwf2g, to be awed by forgiveness.

Schwartz, Martin A., "The Importance of Stupidity in Scientific Research," *Journal of Cell Science*, https://tinyurl.com/ycyxsc95, to be amused and reminded that certainty is rare.

Shah, Khushbu, "There Was a 'Giant Picnic' at the US-Mexico Border," CNN, https://tinyurl.com/y8xs52vh, to see art as invitation, community, protest, and liturgy.

# Videos and Podcasts

Brown, Brené, "The Power of Vulnerability," https://youtu.be/iCvmsMzlF7o, to remember that you are worthy of love and belonging.

Davis, Tanya, "How to Be Alone," https://youtu.be/k7X7sZzSXYs, to learn how to be alone.

Green, John, "How's the Water?" *Vlog Brothers*, https://youtu .be/Qg031UVWrT0, to consider what the water is you're swimming in and the possibility that not knowing is okay.

Jobson, Christopher, "A Floating Coffee Cup Pours a Rainbow of Liquid Pencils," Colossal, https://tinyurl.com/ya3yvpky, to be in awe of what humans can come up with when we experiment.

Joffe-Walt, Chana, "Magic Words: Rainy Days and Mondays," *This American Life*, ep. 532, https://tinyurl.com/ydac2r6l, to ponder how to respond to delusions and to grin.

May, Emmeline, "Tea and Consent," https://youtu.be/pZwvrx VavnQ, to learn what *consent* means clearly and playfully.

Mitchell, David, and Robert Webb, "Are We the Baddies?" https://youtu.be/hn1VxaMEjRU, to laugh a bit and ask yourself the same question.

## Websites

Aluminum Extruded Shapes, http://alum-ext.com, to see some possible shapes extruded in aluminum.

Handspeak, https://tinyurl.com/y7464zd7, to learn the ASL sign for *awkward*.

Moss Wikipedia entry, wikipedia.org/wiki/Moss, to become obsessed with moss along with me.

Project for Awesome, projectforawesome.com, to decrease the suckiness of the world.

## Songs and Poetry

elodieunderglass, "On the Validity of Recognizing Emotions," Tumblr, https://tinyurl.com/y9cda6l4, to be both entertained and convicted by a cartoon swan.

Graves, Robert, "The Naked and the Nude," *The Complete Poems*, to giggle about nudity while feeling quite wise simultaneously.

McCreath, Amy, "What We Need Is Here," https://youtu.be/ZjOrh9naWIc, to be moved by a cappella part-singing.

Peterson, Andrew, "All Shall Be Well," on *The Far Country*, to remember that you are part of something bigger.

Plum Village, established by Thich Nhat Hanh, "Walking Meditation," https://tinyurl.com/y9dl23rg, to learn and practice a new way of being.

Rumi, "The Guest House," in *Open Secret: Versions of Rumi*, trans. John Moyne and Coleman Barks (Boston: Shambhala, 1999), to have your mind blown by a thirteenth-century Sufi mystic.

# NOTES

1. Garbage Oprah, @hannahpaasch, August 6, 2018, https://tinyurl.com/ya5dxjzx.
2. Olga Khazan, "Four Words to Seem More Polite," *The Atlantic*, August 16, 2014, https://tinyurl.com/ycaoyrda.
3. Martin A. Schwartz, "The Importance of Stupidity in Scientific Research," *Journal of Cell Science*, https://tinyurl.com/ycyxsc95.
4. Quoted in Marjorie J. Thompson "Obedience: The Deepest Passion of Love," *Weavings* 3, no. 3 (May/June 1988).
5. Selma Fraiberg, *The Magic Years* (New York: Simon & Schuster, 1987).
6. elodieunderglass, "On the Validity of Recognizing Emotions," Tumblr, https://tinyurl.com/y9cda6l4.
7. Anthony de Mello, *Awareness* (New York: Doubleday, 1990).
8. Katie Couric, "Richmond Police Chief: 'All Lives Matter. That's Really What Community Policing Should Be About,'" Yahoo News, March 22, 2015, https://tinyurl.com/j2m82cz; see also Robert Rogers, "Use of Deadly Force by Police Disappears on Richmond Streets," *East Bay Times*, September 6, 2014, https://tinyurl.com/y76j6xrx.
9. Khushbu Shah, "There Was a 'Giant Picnic' at the US-Mexico Border," CNN, October 11, 2017, https://tinyurl.com/y8xs52vh.
10. Makoto Fujimura, "Consider the Lilies," *Nihonga Notes* (blog), https://tinyurl.com/y7qq9vzc.

11. Lauren F. Friedman and Kevin Loria, "11 Scientific Reasons You Should Be Spending More Time Outside," *Business Insider*, April 22, 2016, https://tinyurl.com/y9wb2mc9.
12. Cara di Silva, ed., *In Memory's Kitchen: A Legacy from the Women of Terezin*, trans. Bianca Steiner Brown (Lanham, MD: Rowman & Littlefield, 1996).

.